GET TO KNOW THE FUTURE—
YOU'RE GOING TO LIVE
YOUR WHOLE LIFE THERE.

"The book is an engagingly written overview of futurist theory today, packed with prophetic scenarios, alternative timetables for the future, and specific predictions about the shape of things to come. There is a chapter on alternative futures ("in which we see that the future is a plural"), a roundup of past visions of tomorrow, such as those of Bellamy, Orwell, and Huxley, and a directory of organizations concerned with the future."

Library Journal

"The book not only tells who is busy looking at the future, but why and, more important, how. . . . Next year you could be making New Year's resolutions for the whole world."

The Washington Post

THE FUTURE FILE

BY PAUL DICKSON

AVON
PUBLISHERS OF BARD, CAMELOT AND DISCUS BOOKS

AVON BOOKS
A division of
The Hearst Corporation
959 Eighth Avenue
New York, New York 10019

Copyright © 1977 by Paul Dickson
Published by arrangement with Rawson Associates Publishers,
Inc.
Library of Congress Catalog Card Number: 77-76998
ISBN 0-380-42242-5

First Avon Printing, February, 1979

AVON TRADEMARK REG. U.S. PAT. OFF. AND IN
OTHER COUNTRIES, MARCA REGISTRADA, HECHO EN
U.S.A.

Printed in the U.S.A.

To the younger readers of this book—
the senior citizens of the early 21st century.

ACKNOWLEDGMENTS

I am indebted to a number of people for their help in the preparation of this book. Those I would like to single out for special thanks are Ed and Sally Cornish of the World Future Society, Willis Harman of the Stanford Research Institute, Alan Ladwig of the Forum for the Advancement of Students in Science and Technology, Inc., and Kent Myers of Futuremics. I also wish to thank those institutions which have permitted me to quote from their studies of the future and to use their scenarios as examples of that futuristic art form. Finally, I am more indebted than ever to Nancy Dickson for her aid and comfort.

CONTENTS

II

Almanac and Directory

THE STATE OF THE FUTURE

I

THE TOMORROWS BUSINESS

An Introduction to the Future

A group of think-tank researchers in Menlo Park, California, have come up with a collection of ten alternative future scenarios for the United States between now and the year 2000. In nine out of ten of them, profound social change takes place, reversing trends which have long been taken for granted. Some are downright disastrous.

Meanwhile, the National Aeronautics and Space Administration is looking at the possibility of bringing asteroids back from deep space, placing them in earth orbit, and mining them from large spacecraft. By NASA's reckoning, an asteroid one kilometer in diameter contains four billion tons of high quality steel which is worth about $400 billion in current dollars.

A computer that is now in operation at the Urban Institute in Washington, D.C., is able to advance the course of the lives of several thousand living Americans ahead through the year 2000. Inside this remarkable machine the inhabitants have children, move, divorce and remarry, retire and die—all in the years ahead. The purpose of this unique exercise is to test future social programs and trends to see what effect such things will have on you and me.

The Futures Group, an unusual consulting firm based in Glastonbury, Connecticut, gathers and collects specific predictions about the next fifty years for its powerful clients from all over the world who are interested in how it can help them plan for the future using the group's more than 60,000 predictions.

These are but a few of many examples of a dynamic development known as futurism. It has been called the fastest-growing educational phenomenon in history, the most important new concept to hit government in a hundred years, an invaluable tool for industry, and a major breakthrough in human thinking.

Its growth is awesome. A university survey group has concluded that there are now more than 3,000 courses offered in futurism in the United States alone; the Washington-based World Futures Society now boasts 20,000 dues-paying members, and just one company that does futures research has served more than 500 corporate and government clients to date. Futures research has become a multimillion-dollar-a-year growth industry—despite the fact that it produces goods no more durable than forecasts, alternative images of the future, and carefully extrapolated statistics on the year 2000. Everybody seems to be getting into the futures research act: federal agencies do it, states do it, and even the city of Columbus, Indiana (population under 20,000), does it—to say nothing of the United Nations, the U.S. Congress, and nations as diverse as Korea, Poland, and Sweden. The Library of Congress has estimated that close to 100 private research institutes and think tanks in the United States alone are involved in some aspect of futures research.

Meanwhile, the future has become one of the hottest items on the lecture circuit since William Jennings Bryan made the rounds. It is the inspiration for several hundred recent books (on the future of everything from medicine to leisure) and the basis for things as diverse as conferences, magazines and journals, games, and a growing number of citizen-based future-planning groups.

The idea of looking ahead to the future is hardly a new one—it dates back to the ancient oracles and portent readers who claimed they could divine the future by studying signs manifested in the entrails of animals. In its modern incarnation, portents come from the entrails of computers or from packs of experts assembled into "Delphi panels." This modern futurism got its feet in the 1960s, gathered speed in the early 1970s, and is now on the verge of becoming supersonic.

Despite this tremendous growth, however, it is still accurate to say that the art is primarily practiced by those who are clustered away in think tanks, government policy research groups, university computing centers, and the deep-pile carpeted dens of corporation headquarters. This means that some of the most important forecasts, future options, and alternative images of the tomorrow that are now being laid out for us tend to get locked up in obscure reports, windy memos, expensive seminars, and computer print-outs.

What follows is an attempt to help pull futurism out of the Olympian realm where it now resides and hasten its transfer into the public domain. This seems altogether proper because while we are pretty much stuck with the present, there is every reason to believe we can and should have an effect on the future, rather than have it entirely managed for us by others. This echoes the thought behind the most famous of all lines about the future, a quote from the inventor C. F. Kettering, which says, "My interest is in the future, because I'm going to spend the rest of my life there."

To do this, the book has been assembled in two main sections. The first is an overview of today's futurism and the futurists, featuring the kinds of driving ideas, personalities, envisioned worlds, concepts of the future, and specific forecasts that make the whole business tick. This overview section will open with a short history of the future, have as its finale a collection of specific, authoritative predictions about the future laid out in timetable fashion, and, in between, discuss examples like those that were mentioned at the beginning of the chapter.

The second part will be an almanac and directory of the future, pointing to diverse opportunities for further futuristic involvement and thinking. Included will be a "yellow pages" of futures groups and associations, sources of futuristic games, important charts about the future, models for helping you write your own future scenarios, and even a collection of the worst predictions of all times. This section is based on the premise that a futurist is a person who decides to become one and is meant to give the information needed to achieve that end.

Before getting underway, however, there are some general observations on the art of futurism and the future itself which should be made at the outset. These are the basic premises and conclusions of the book, which draw heavily on current futurist thinking. They are listed in no special order and are simply intended to give a quick fix on the subject at hand.

• The future is unknowable in advance—however, various future developments and possibilities are predictable.
• The most fundamental tenet of futurism is that we are, to a large degree, creating the future right now with our present decisions, discoveries, policies, actions and inactions.
• Since the future is not inevitable, one of the few things that virtually all futurists believe is that there is a broad array of *alternative futures* open to us. It therefore follows that the proper role of futurism is to lay out these alternatives for present inspection. The point of the whole exercise, of course, is to avoid the undesirable futures and move toward the most desirable one.
• A futurist does not aim to predict the future as such (although specific events and innovations may be forecast) but rather tries to lay out an assortment of possible futures. Each future is examined to see what policies, events, and attitudes would lead to its realization.
• There is a major difference between a prediction (or forecast) and a list of alternative futures. Generally, futurists use the former to state the probability of a specific event or development taking place (such as the approximate date when the population of China will exceed one billion people), while the latter is used to explore broad social, economic, and political changes (such as the possible state of American agriculture in the year 2000).
• A prediction that does not come true is not necessarily a bad prediction. For instance, predictions that have fore-

told environmental catastrophe may be avoided in the long run because of those very predictions. To put it more dramatically, the accuracy of a future forecast is trivial compared to its impact on the present.

• Futurism is basically a *surprise-free* proposition—that is, predictions that become realities do not surprise their authors, even if the odds are against them taking place. The "legionnaires' disease" was a surprise, but the first heart transplant was not for the simple reason that doctors had been working on organ transplants for some time.

• While futurists believe that surprises by their very nature are unpredictable, they contend that we have to learn to prepare for and cope with them. A futurist looks at the first Arab oil boycott (a surprise) and attempts to prepare for the possibility of a second (less of a surprise).

• Despite its academic trappings, futurism is basically action-oriented, in that it is ultimately geared to creating the future rather than simply thinking about what it will be like.

• There is a fundamental difference between traditional long-range planning and futurism. The planner generally extrapolates from the present and the past, while the futurist attempts to look at all the reasonable possibilities. For instance, a planner looks at birth statistics to determine the future need for hospital beds in an area; the futurist asks if there are better options to the present concept of patient care or innovations on the horizon which could change the demand for hospital beds, such as electronic monitoring devices that will allow a patient to be diagnosed at home as his heartbeat, blood count, and other variables are telegraphed to the hospital.

• Futurists have more separate visions of the future world than cab drivers have of what is wrong with the present one. Anyone looking for a unified view of the future should keep in mind that futurists can't even decide on a common name for what they do and still debate over whether it should be called futurism, futurology, futuristics, predictive study, prognostics, prevision, etc.

• As a discipline, futurism is still very much in its infancy.

As a field of human activity, it is as much beset by irrelevancies, feuds, blatant subjectivism, and problems as any other (which also helps make it interesting).

• Up to this point, futurism has primarily been geared to helping the big institutions, but it is becoming increasingly apparent that the average person can benefit from futurism, a point that this book attempts to further.

2

A CONCISE HISTORY OF THE FUTURE

A Look at Bygone Futures Which Demonstrate the Wisdom of Arthur C. Clarke's Oft-Quoted Line, "The future ain't what it used to be."

In the bluntest of terms the future we're supposed to be on the verge of entering has disappeared.

All one has to do is to think back to the plans and goals of recent times to see this. If things had worked out the way the nation's planners and leaders had hoped, the war on poverty would have been long-won, there would be a superabundance of energy, crime would be on the wane, our cities would be revitalized, the world would be well fed, and government would be humming along as a model of efficiency and good service to the people—to name just a few plans gone awry.

Instead we are in a time of surprise, mixed blessings, shortages, and, most of all, confusion. Traditional planning, faith in science, and the concept of a limitless earth have all been deeply shaken. The situation is best described by small but telling examples, of which there seem to be a limitless supply. The following does the job as well as any, however: with some true idealism, we created the Consumer Product Safety Commission to help protect us from our own technology. That group righteously tried to reduce infant deaths by banning flammable sleepwear for little children and then discovered that some of the new nonflammable fabrics it had substituted for the old flammable ones cause cancer.

In addition to the scads of contemporary examples, there are others shaping up for the years ahead. A decade ago the American Social Security System had virtually no critics and was thought of as a permanent working institution with no built-in flaws. Now we are being told that we may be heading for a day early in the 21st century when the children of the baby boom retire and their children may have to pay up to 50 percent of their income just to keep the system in operation. The question is, of course, will today's children be willing to foot that bill—no small matter for those now working who are planning their lives on the assumption that the system will remain in operation. There could be a sad irony awaiting those now in their twenties who pay for their parents' generation's retirement and their children's generation's education only to end up with a defunct retirement system in the year 2008.

For the simple reason that the future appears to be as elusive and unclear as it has ever been, futurism is on the rise and futurists are dwelling on the meaning of cases like those of the flammable pajamas and the future of Social Security (both are in fact under study at the Center for Futures Research at the University of Southern California).

All of this calls for a flashback to see how we got to our present state of the future.

Human beings have been trying to get a grip on their future since the beginnings of recorded history. The oracles of ancient Greece, the prophecies of the Bible, portent readers from many cultures, medieval seers, astrologists past and present, and rustics with divining rods are all cases in point.

For centuries, writers and philosophers have been challenged by the notion of describing the world to come, with Leonardo da Vinci, Francis Bacon, Voltaire, Hans Christian Andersen, and Jules Verne among the many who rose to the challenge. Of all of these, Voltaire may have been the first to suggest the modern idea of exploring alternative futures, as opposed to simply predicting the future. During the 19th century and for a good part of the 20th, the major source of future thinking was from writers who became fascinated with what might be and put it down on paper as thought-provoking fiction.

BELLAMY AND WELLS

Clearly the most important 19th-century exercise in futurism was Edward Bellamy's *Looking Backward, 2000–1887*, a novel in which the author wakes up in the year 2000 after a long hypnotic sleep to describe the world around him. The book is still in print today, but it is pretty tame reading for the simple reason that so many of his ideas are already or will soon be taken for granted. He described electric lights, equal rights and job status for women, radio and television (he called it an "electro-scope"), nonpolluting vehicles, electric stoves, the use of private aircraft, labor-saving appliances for the home, and more. Some of the social issues he discussed actually sound like they were snatched out of the newspapers of the 1970s: "full employment," "the right of the unborn" to equal rights for education and personal development, and a guaranteed annual income. Even his misses tend to be near-misses. For example, his vision of solid waste being electrically cremated will probably not come to pass as such, but the idea shows that he was thinking about the future problem of solid waste disposal.

When the book first appeared, it was termed preposterous by some reviewers (the Boston *Transcript* said the book could have had merit if it were set seventy-five centuries in the future rather than 113 years), but it had tremendous popular appeal. Hundreds of thousands of copies were sold, and Bellamy clubs and societies sprang up all over the nation to study and advance the ideas in Bellamy's Utopia. Not long ago a group at Columbia University looked back at the literature of the last hundred years to judge what had had the greatest influence on world thought and finally concluded that Bellamy's writings were second in importance only to those of Karl Marx.

Because of Bellamy's ability to foresee specific new

inventions and social change, people sometimes forget the kind of overall society he envisioned. He had a naïve fascination and faith in massive and powerful bureaucracies managed with totalitarian efficiency. Lewis Mumford had termed this side of Bellamy's vision as that of the "archetypal megamachine," previewing to various degrees the rise of Nazism, Russian communism, and the Western welfare state. His vision was correct, but his expectation of an ideal state was far off the mark.

While *Looking Backward* is still well remembered, his short stories are not. However, they are important because he used them to explore the outer reaches of scientific thought and conjecture, which, again, put him way ahead of his time. His stories prefigure late 20th-century fascination with ESP, altered states of consciousness, psychokinesis, time travel, nonverbal communication, and extraterrestrial life. In a piece entitled "Dr. Heidenhoff's Process," he envisions a form of medicine in which people whose lives have been wrecked by past traumas can be freed from them. Save for the fact that Bellamy's process involves the use of a "galvanic-mesmeric device," his Dr. Heidenhoff sounds a lot like Dr. Freud.

Just as Bellamy's life was coming to an end, a young Englishman named H. G. Wells came along and seemed to pick up where Bellamy left off by creating new scientific fantasies, Utopias, and lists of inventions yet to come. Wells's fame as a predictor is so well known that it is enough to say that he was able to describe a vast array of later developments, including the atomic bomb, the military use of aircraft, and the armor-plated military tank. He also showed an amazing ability to pick dates, such as when, in 1933, he not only anticipated World War II, but was only a few months off in predicting its beginning. Wells, like Bellamy, was also a utopian who forecast and argued in behalf of a worldwide "New Republic" (or "Modern Utopia") which would be peaceful and prosperous, but also rigid. Wells talked of a planetary caste system managed by technicians. The caste system would be run with Samurai-like severity, and it would actually be illegal to mate outside of one's class, thereby making this ideal world one with more than passing resemblance to the feudal past.

If the Utopias of Bellamy and Wells were far from perfect, their urge to create a future world to think about before it was created had great influence on the thinking of others. This was particularly true when they talked about the consequences of new inventions, which both men correctly reasoned were to come along at an alarming speed. Unlike true scientists who stopped at the point where facts were known, Bellamy, Wells, Verne, and others thought nothing of fabricating a detail to get us from the present to the future. Wells, therefore, was able to invent the atomic bomb on paper by making up a name for the substance needed to charge the explosion. He called it carolinium, which meant he did not have to wait for the discovery of plutonium to write about nuclear warfare. Significantly, in 1934 when the pioneer nuclear scientist Leo Szilard realized how a chain reaction could be touched off, he immediately realized the implications of his discovery and moved to keep it out of the public domain. As he wrote many years later, he knew those implications in 1934 because he had read H. G. Wells.

The tradition established by these writers lives on in the form of the modern science fiction writers who have hit on some remarkably accurate predictions. For instance, in 1945 Arthur C. Clarke described perfectly the communications satellite—thirteen years before the first one was developed; and in 1941 Robert Heinlein published a story called "Solution Unsatisfactory" in which the United States stages a great research program to develop an atomic bomb and that program leads other nations to do the same, ultimately leading to an international nuclear stalemate.

The fact that some of these predictions come true is just part of the story. Often these writers use fiction to predict either developments they hope will not come true or side effects of a development they are telling us to avoid. This is one of the main reasons why rosy predictions do disservice to the future. Isaac Asimov has pointed out that while Wells as well as other lesser-known writers predicted the coming of the automotive age with astonishing clarity, little thought was given to the traffic jams and pollution that were to come with it. Asimov contends that if a writer in the 1880s had written a popular novel that drove home these negative points, it could have had impact on the design of cities and created a much earlier awareness of the dangers of pollution.

For this very reason, the various futures to be avoided have become the strongest themes in 20th-century predictive fiction. Books like *1984, Brave New World, A Clockwork Orange, The Wanting Seed, The Eco-Spasm Report, On the Beach,* and many more are much more compelling and important reading than books which describe Utopias.

THE OFFICIAL FUTURE

Throughout history fiction writers were not alone in their discovery of the future as a realm for conjecture. Scholars, industrialists, and government officials were also taking their own flings into the world to come. One of the most fascinating examples of early futurism of this type came in the form of a study commissioned by Louis XV. The king asked J. L. Favier, a scholar, to look at the alternative futures that the French monarchy was likely to face. His report was delivered in 1773 and was well received, but was soon found to contain one major oversight: the French Revolution.

There were a number of other studies over the years, but the first truly major organized look at the future in modern times was that contained in the report of the President's Panel on Recent Social Trends, a product of the Hoover Administration in 1929. It made a number of forecasts, many of which were right on target, but missed one key point: it failed to acknowledge that the nation was moving into a long, debilitating depression (although it did talk about some of the problems which caused it). If nothing else, this was in keeping with the forced optimism of the times. Indeed, Hoover continually talked about a rapid recovery from the time of the market crash through the election of 1932, when he was defeated by Franklin D. Roosevelt.

Despite its one major shortcoming, the "Trends" report was of great significance in putting the future on a new footing as a proper concern of the American government and the academic community. In its wake came all sorts of essays and high-toned articles on the future, with many of these efforts falling far below that of the Hoover commission.

In 1931, for instance, *The Scientific Monthly* commissioned leading experts in genetics, sociology, and archaeology to predict the future from the perspectives of their specialties. Collectively, they hit on a few good predictions (birth control pills, the coming of the age of big business, government and labor, and the boom in electrical appliances for the home), but otherwise they blew it. Interest in human contraception was growing in 1931, which led to the prediction that world population growth was slowing and might even decline in the years ahead. In fact, the geneticist looked at current trends and confidently predicted that the world's population would not reach 3.5 billion until the year 2530, when in actuality it is now over 4 billion. The same Harvard geneticist also reported that blacks and American Indians would disappear as racial entities with their remnants being absorbed by the "superior" white race. His reasoning was that white progress in the colonial development of Africa and South America would force the "inferior races" into a struggle with whites which they would naturally lose. Just as the future did not bode well for the "inferior races," it also looked bleak for the "inferior sex," which would have an increasingly tough time with male technology. Women, we were told, had still not mastered the art of opening a tin can. Also foretold were: a single worldwide language brought about by the miracle of radio, a quick end to world poverty, and a new caste system based on genetic quality. The concept of atomic energy, on the other hand, was branded as "nonsensical."

Writing of this type tended to prove that those under the strong spell of a particular discipline or school of thought were apt to have more influence than those who were less dogmatic. Consequently there were and are Freudian, Marxist, and capitalistic views of the years ahead, which differ significantly and can be equally influential. In the 1930s and earlier, for instance, Darwin's influence was so strong that when scientists talked about the future, they sometimes went so far as to suggest that medical and humanitarian concern with saving sickly infants was ill advised because it could weaken the human race and ultimately force a regression to apelike primitivism or worse. The eminent English scientist J. B. S. Haldane in his 1928 book *Possible Worlds* offered this view of the future if man did not manage his own evolution:

It is quite likely that, after a golden age of happiness and peace, during which all of the immediate benefits of science will be realized, mankind will gradually deteriorate . . . and in a few thousand or a few hundred years—it does not matter which—mankind will return to barbarism, and finally become extinct.

Haldane and other scientist talked of ideal eugenic states of the future in which the intelligent people would breed and means would be found to keep the unintelligent from having children. Some actually talked about VD, knife-fighting among young men of the lower classes, infant mortality, and the like as being genetically beneficial.

Eugenics aside, another major factor which came into play in the thirties was the advent of Franklin D. Roosevelt and the New Deal, which brought with it an unprecedented concern for planning, relief, and regulation. Like it or not, it was quickly apparent to most Americans that the nation was now in the hands of a man who thought in long-range terms, offered programmatic solutions to problems, and advocated a strong central government able to shape the nation's future. Roosevelt and his brain trust were doing precisely what a leading member of that brain trust, Rexford G. Tugwell, had envisioned in a few lines of free verse that he had written years before FDR was elected:

I have gathered my tools and my charts;
My plans are fashioned and practical;
I shall roll up my sleeves—
                make America over!

Not surprisingly, in the late 1930s there was an intense flurry of popular interest in the future, which resulted in several studies by blue ribbon panels of experts, a number of magazine and newspaper articles in which the future was envisioned, and the "World of Tomorrow" theme of the 1939 World's Fair in Flushing Meadow, New York— "the microcosm of all phases of future life," said the event's promoters.

Looking back at the futurism of this period, one finds that the era's vision of tomorrow was dominated by lists of inventions that would touch on the life of the average person, new consumer goods, and an ever-increasing improvement in the quality of life. The concern for materialism and a better life is easily understood, for these predictions were being cast at the end of the great depression.

If one excludes some of the quaint terminology (for instance, a prediction that foresaw an "electric pig" in every kitchen was actually talking about garbage disposal units), it is remarkable how many of both the short-term and far-out predictions came true. Here are just a few of the predictions that were common during the time, showing up in a variety of places ranging from the Sunday supplements of the newspapers to the august Report on Technological Trends and National Policy of the National Resources Committee:

The widespread use of air conditioning

3-D movies

"Electric eye" door openers and security devices

Direct intercontinental telephone dialing

Frozen food

Plastic furniture and a host of other commonplace items from the new technology of plastics

An increasing development of and reliance on synthetic textiles

Prefabricated housing

Multichannel television in operation from coast to coast, both in terms of traditional broadcasting and cable transmission

One detailed example of the period's futurecasting appeared in an article in *Harper's Monthly* for March, 1938, in which writer Arthur Train, Jr., borrowed from some of the then-current future studies to describe a day in the life of one John Doe in the year 1988. Some of the narrative dwells on developments realized long ago (clock radios, home air filtration and air conditioning, the pocket tape recorder and pocket camera, the tape library, and even plastic knick-knacks and ashtrays), while there are others that it is hard to imagine at this point will be ready for 1988 (like the Doe family's collection of steep-takeoff aircraft parked on the family roof). But much of it seems to hold up as an image of what 1988 might actually be like, such as this description of the Does' neighborhood and home:

His house was situated at a considerable distance from the city, in an "integrated" neighborhood which had been carefully planned by a city planning board. The houses were grouped about a park, and in addition to the school and library there was a central air-conditioning plant and a community center with a television transmission set, an auditorium whose television receiving set boasted color and three-dimensional sound and sight, a trailer camp, all kinds of recreational facilities, the vegetable factory, the poultry factory, and the plant where garbage was converted into fertilizer.

The house itself was somewhat smaller and had smaller rooms than one would have expected of a man with Mr. Doe's means. The large custom-built house had long ago gone the way of the large custom-built automobile. It was a long, low, flat-roofed building made up of a cluster of prefabricated units whose irregular arrangement prevented it from looking monotonous. Unlike the houses of the early part of the century and all preceding eras, whose aim was to give an impression of volume, the whole building was so translucent, neutral, and fragile-looking, so broken into planes by terraces and porches, that it gave the impression of being no more than part of the out-of-doors which had been etched into the frame with a few strokes of a sharp pointed pencil.

In the construction of the house the use of wood, bricks, and plaster had practically been superseded by panels of beryllium and magnesium alloys; low-grade silicas, or glass-like materials; sheet materials such as asbestos cement, and occasionally plastic. . . . A considerable use was made of moving partitions which made it possible to enclose a small space when privacy was required, and still provide a large space when it was not. The insulation, of "mineral fluff," was of course built into the prefabricated panels.

In the various rooms many of the pieces of furniture were made of plastic molded as a unit, while others were made of magnesium alloy. In place of cushions, spongelike synthetic upholstery was used.

Ironically, however, the writer tells us that David Sarnoff's 1936 prediction of cheap portable radios for instant communication with others (a very accurate description of the CB radio) would not be realized by 1988. He also went on to categorize predictions about death rays, rocket planes, germ warfare, and trips to the moon as being lurid, sensational, and irresponsible.

Written descriptions of the future were one thing, but if you wanted to see it all jell and come together in one place, the 1939 World's Fair was the place to go. By visiting exhibits like Ford's "Road of Tomorrow," General Motors' "Futurama," the multisponsored "Town of Tomorrow" exhibit, and the Fair's centerpiece display "Democracity," the future realities of superhighways, ranch houses, rec rooms, and home workshops for "do-it yourselfers," booming suburbs (or "satellites to Democracity") replete with large developments of prefabricated houses, two-car garages for two-car families, stereo sound, and so much more were all on display. The displays were collectively so complete that one could find working models of such things as "the Dairy Farm of the Future," "the Drug Store of Tomorrow," and "the Bottling Plant of the Future." For millions of Americans abstract promises were rendered tangible, and the official guidebook to the Fair was able to boast, for instance, that television was "actually demonstrated" at the RCA exhibit.

For a glimpse of an even further-out future, you could look at General Electric's solar power display, Westinghouse's working robot, and the Transportation Pavilion's area devoted to space exploration. To their credit, Fair planners saved a little room for some of the problems of the future: at the central food exhibit there was an area devoted to "the challenge to the future," which emphasized a decreasing ability to feed the world's increasing population as the 20th century wore on. There was also a major display on American poverty billed as a problem needing a solution in the near future.

Beyond the actual exhibits, there were those who looked at the event and at the millions who attended, and proclaimed the whole thing evidence of a new quest for recreation and leisure that would take on tremendous importance in the years ahead.

As it turned out, the world of tomorrow of the late 1930s had to be the day after tomorrow because of World War II, but the dream was carried intact into the late 1940s and early 1950s when it began to be realized.

BATTING AVERAGES

Before moving on to futurism in the modern era it is worth asking how the earlier technological forecasters did with their specific predictions. George Wise of the General Electric Research and Development Center collected 1,556 predictions made publicly by Americans (inventors, writers, industrialists, etc.) between the years 1890 and 1940 and sorted them into four classes: fulfilled, in progress (the development is evident but not fully established), not proven (but not proven impossible either), and refuted. The results of this work, reported in the magazine *Futures* in October, 1976, was that less than half of the predictions had been fulfilled or were in the process of being fulfilled. A full third had been refuted.

Wise found that the "batting averages" (the number of right predictions divided by the total number of predictions) was significantly better for experts (.444) than for nonexperts (.336). Individual batting averages ranged widely from the .800 average of inventor Charles Kettering to that of Henry Ford, who completely struck out with a flat .000. Thomas Edison posted a very respectable .588 and engineer-inventor Charles Steinmetz averaged .360.

THE ATOMIC FUTURE

Because it was a time of great stress, the period during World War II afforded little opportunity for thinking about any aspect of the future save for winning and getting back to normal when it was all over. For those waging the war the image of the future was commonly expressed in terms of the simplest of things: homemade apple pie, a well-paying nine-to-five job, and a new car.

But when the industrialized world came out of the war, its leaders were confronted with a totally new situation. Because of the development of the A-bomb, humans now had the power to inflict tremendous damage on the planet and, as the nuclear and thermonuclear stockpile grew, to destroy it entirely. For the first time in history, it was possible to wipe out the future.

With that apocalyptic thought in mind, the period was also one of prosperity, the growth of government, organized science and industry, and increasing consumer comfort. The times clearly called for new institutions and new ways of looking at things which acknowledged the need for forecasting, planning, regulation, and thinking in larger terms, rather than the less organized prediction that went on in the past. Dennis Little, the futurist who heads the

Futures Research Unit at the Library of Congress, has studied this period from 1945 to 1950 and can tick off some of the evidence of this trend, which he says includes the new concept of the Gross National Product, the formation of such government agencies as the National Science Foundation and the Atomic Energy Commission, the Full Employment Act of 1947, and the appearance of think tanks to do long-range planning for government and industry.

It was not as if there were a master plan for the future or anything so unified, but that things seemed more manageable with the aid of existing institutions and new programs. When the decision was made to help rebuild war-devastated Europe, the Marshall Plan was framed, put into operation, and was soon working. The common desire to prevent another world war was expressed in the formation of the United Nations, which was born with the greatest of optimism, and even the atomic bomb was spoken of as the mushroom cloud with a silver lining as experts began talking of the coming age of nuclear energy, which would provide us with electricity that would be too cheap to even bother metering.

The future was something subject to logical control and the 1950s bore this out, as few developments were truly shocking but rather the result of inevitable social, technical, and political developments. The Cold War seemed a rational alternative to hot war, NATO and SEATO were logical alliances, and there was hope in the disarmament conferences which were getting underway. The atomic submarine, the Salk vaccine, the growth in computing power, and an airplane able to go 1,600 miles per hour were among the many developments that proved that science and technology were bearing the fruit of heavy investment.

Even those events which should have tipped everyone off to the social changes to come, such as the *Brown* v. *Board of Education* decision and the first civil rights sit-ins, did not shatter the calm of the period. That came later.

This is not to say that there were no surprises. The October 4, 1957, launch of the Soviet Sputnik 1 amounted to a technological Pearl Harbor for America, and was profoundly disturbing to those in power. Within weeks, America's scientific superiority, its educational system, and even its ability to defend itself were called into question. The response to this was the Soviet-American space race, an unprecedented area for international competition, but still a logical extension of the Cold War arms race. The idea of landing humans on the moon was an exciting prospect, but one which people took in stride and saw as having little direct impact on their lives.

If there was a single statement that characterized the 1950s and its view of the fuure, it was the report of President Eisenhower's Commission on National Goals. Issued in final form in 1960, this was a presidential attempt to have a nonpartisan group of top leaders and thinkers map out a plan for the coming decade. In all, some fifteen major goals were spelled out. Most of them sound remarkably familiar almost twenty years later, as they are precisely the points that today's politicians talk about achieving in the future: tax reform, an improved quality of education, the avoidance of inflation, full employment, a more efficient agricultural system, improved health care at lower personal cost, a reduced balance of foreign payments, a strengthened United Nations, the need for nuclear disarmament, and so forth. While a few have largely been realized, namely, higher pay for federal workers, reduced discrimination, and greater support of science, the goals for the 1960s were basically those that would sound nice for any modern decade, including the 1980s, and in reality describe an American Utopia—a booming, inflationless, efficient, and equitable society.

ENTER THE 1960s

For a number of reasons the next decade's future did not work out the way it was supposed to. The image held in the calm days of the late 1950s and the early days of the 1960s was a rather neat one. An adventuresome race to the moon was on and there was serious talk of true nuclear arms control. It was a time of idealism typified by the Peace Corps and John F. Kennedy's inaugural call for a struggle to eliminate ". . . tyranny, poverty, disease and war itself." American science and technology had recovered from the shock of Sputnik and were again promising a bountiful array of new concepts, discoveries, and goods.

The Kennedy assassination in 1963, the Watts eruption in 1965, the little war in Vietnam that kept getting bigger, and so much else that followed blew a jagged, irreparable hole in the image. And on closer examination the promise of new invention did not seem as attractive or attainable as it had looked at first glance. Before long, a sad quip was going around Washington that a new presidential commission would soon be started to find out what had happened to the report of the presidential commission on National Goals.

It is interesting to compare the New York World's Fair of 1964/1965, which proclaimed itself "An Olympics of Progress," with its vision of the future, to the 1939 World of Tomorrow affair. General Motors updated its 1939 exhibit in a new Futurama which contained such things as submarine sports cars for visiting plush underwater resort hotels, superskyscrapers, midtown vertical takeoff jetports, intercontinental highways, and jungles transformed into metropolises in a matter of weeks. Other displays featured cars riding on air cushions, interplanetary recreational travel, weightless orbiting as a new sport, thermonuclear power (as opposed to plain old nuclear power), and, in several displays, bubble-topped climatically controlled cities with conveyor-belt sidewalks. There was an all-electric city of the future and a futuristic natural gas pavillion (with the ironic motto "Gas is the energy of the future"), which included the Kitchen of the Future, a sleek Rube Goldberg affair where all sorts of gas-fueled appliances automatically popped in and out of walls, floors, and ceilings as they were needed.

With many of the dreams of the 1939 Fair now realized, this Fair seemed to be taking those old dreams and trying to push them to new and often absurd levels. This absurdity was perhaps best exemplified by the image of the variously heated or air-conditioned bubble city with its ever-moving sidewalks which turned walking into an assembly-line operation for the production of weak hearts. An absurdity of near-equal rank, however, was the exhibitor's compulsion to render things bigger, faster, and more automated. The Chrysler exhibit, for instance, not only featured the world's largest car (80 feet long) but a gargantuan assembly line.

A dozen years later the future of that Fair seems as quaint and remote as a Victorian image of the future. In no special order, the 1964 image was done in by: the seemingly endless Vietnam War, the environmental awakening of the late 1960s, inflation, the natural gas crisis, the Arab oil boycott, the urban disorders of the late 1960s, the financial problems of the cities in the 1970s, the 55-mile-per-hour speed limit, the nuclear power debate, and more. New York City not only lacks a bubble but hardly has enough money to patch its old sidewalks, let alone install moving ones. The same newspapers that were awed by the superskyscrapers, subsonic turbine cars, and electronically managed farms envisioned in 1964 are now cueing editorials around themes like "small is beautiful" and "limits to growth."

As always, in retrospect some visions and predictions fared better than others. Those in the 1960s who forecast such things as quantum jumps in computer speeds, organ transplants and other medical achievements, a successful moon landing, tremendous growth in satellite communications, and other technical advances tended to have good batting averages.

THE SOARING SEVENTIES?

While the 1970s have not been marked by the same unexpected social change and upheaval that beset the 1960s, the decade thus far has again been one in which the vision held at the beginning was not borne out by its reality.

In fact, in terms of the history of the future the decade

started out on a rather telling level in 1970 with the release of the White House study on "Goals for Americans," which had been started in 1969 by Leonard Garment, Daniel P. Moynihan, and Richard Nixon. The White House billed it as a major look ahead at the nation's trends and possibilities and released it with great fanfare. It was a total failure. It not only avoided most of the major issues for the future (foreign policy, the war, health, housing, crime, race relations, and the plight of the cities were among the items not discussed), but the issues it did confront were loaded with self-serving comments on administration plans and policies. Moreover, people who worked on the report complained that men with blue pencils close to the President had edited out all sorts of relevant details, such as taking out all references to Ralph Nader in the discussion of the future of consumerism, choosing instead to mention consumer advocates who were little known then and little known now. Furthermore, as with Louis XV's future without a revolution and Hoover's future without a depression, Nixon's future study did not hint at the future he was to create for himself.

Reaction to the report was so negative that it was soon forgotten. One of the few reviews of the study which did not call it dull, dishonest, or both appeared in the Washington *Post*. That review was written by Ken W. Clawson, who was later to leave the paper to become a post-Watergate apologist for the Nixon White House. In Contrast, the Washington *Star*'s William Hines had this to say about the report: "A blue-covered National Goals report, delivered to President Nixon the other day with fanfare appropriate to bringing the tablets from Sinai, is a bagful of wind."

During the same year that the generally long-forgotten Goals Report was issued, others were trying to get a quick fix on the decade just starting. There seemed to be an urge on the part of many to put the nation on a new footing with projections for stunning accomplishments for what some of them tried to tab the "Soaring Seventies." A 1970 conference sponsored by the Polytechnic Institute of Brooklyn, entitled "Technology Forecast for 1980," drew a bunch of experts together who predicted such specifics for the end of the decade as:

—Automated highways on which cars will travel at high speeds on computerized pallets without driver control

—Undersea hotels and resorts

—Ready-to-inhabit homes delivered by helicopters

—Television-computer watchdogs to *drastically* cut crime by catching bank robbers, car thieves, and the like before they can complete their act

—The emergence of new power sources, cryogenics for one, that will be supplying the electricity needed for an expanding world economy

—The ability to control (or at least modify) hurricanes and other severe weather

—The widespread ability to stimulate the pleasure centers of the brain for sensual recreation

Although we are still a few years short of the delivery date for these developments, there is little basis to believe that even one of them will have occurred by 1980.

There were other big thoughts on the 1970s which even included fashions. In *Life*'s big 1970 double issue on the decade ahead, Rudi Gernreich told us that in a few years we would all be wearing cheap, lightweight, altogether unisex, synthetic knit clothing which would be disposable after one wearing. Neither males nor females would wear tops when it was warm, and when there was a little nip in the air "see through" tops would be worn.

As it turned out, of course, Gernreich's fashions have not come into vogue—nor do they look like they have much of a chance in a world where thermostats are set at 55 degrees at night and in which disposable knit clothing would represent a massive waste of energy and resources.

More important, there was also a widespread assumption that developed in the late 1960s and early days of the 1970s that many of America's and the world's problems would be solved during the decade as the best brains and technology got to work on them. The rallying cry came on the heels of the 1971 moon landing. It was reasoned that if men could be put on the moon, other great feats could be accomplished, such as revitalizing the cities, turning crime rates back, finding new sources of food, curbing the narcotics plague, and so forth. In certain areas, like cleaning up the environment, advances were made, but in others the solutions simply were not to come.

THE SOLUTION PROBLEM

As if the problems were not enough, in too many cases the "solutions" did little more than create new ones There have been dozens of examples, but just a few are enough to make the point: Addictive heroin was attacked with addictive methadone . . . The old post office system was dismantled because it was a billion dollars in the red and in its place we got a "businesslike" postal service which is now racking up a $3 billion annual deficit and cutting back on services to boot . . . Giant public housing complexes were built but quickly turned into high-rise ghettos because nobody created new job opportunities to go with them . . . Gargantuan federal agencies like HUD and HEW were created to streamline services and instead became vast bureaucracies wrapped in red tape . . . The War on Poverty dwindled down to a mere skirmish, which appears to have been won by the consultants and administrators paid to run it . . . The United States developed a highly sophisticated apparatus for preventing farmers from growing certain crops, which was perfected just before the world hunger problem became evident . . . The criminal justice system was liberalized, from bail to sentencing, without paying much attention to rehabilitation and recidivism . . . And we made marvelous plans for the future of our cities without bothering to figure out where the money would come from.

Even the ability to regulate came into question, as these examples from a recent report from the U.S.C. Center for Futures Research so bluntly demonstrates:

● The Civil Aeronautics Board, originally intended to keep (a) airlines healthy and (b) customers well served through low prices now does neither. Perversely, it now causes many airlines to run in the red while driving up prices for passengers.

• The Interstate Commerce Commission, intended to regulate railroads for the benefit of consumers, now serves the interests of the trucking industry at the expense of railroads and consumers.

• U.S. government efforts over the last twenty years, intended to keep the price of energy artificially low, led many industries to view energy as a "free good." Consequently, they invested heavily in energy-intensive technologies that are suddenly becoming inefficient as energy prices soar.

What is more, some of the very institutions that were created to anticipate problems and events are badly failing to keep track of future reality. The 1975 hearings of the House Select Committee on Intelligence revealed, for example, that the Central Intelligence Agency, which spends unaccounted millions trying to get an advance warning of world events, had failed to predict such turning points as the Tet Offensive in Vietnam, the Cyprus crisis, the 1973 Yom Kippur War, and the 1974 coup in Portugal. Closer to home, government attempts to predict the nation's occupational needs for the future have been a consistent, long-range failure leading to situations in which people are trained for jobs that don't exist and creating shortages in fields where more are needed. This is manifested by the fact that we are now in a period when there are too many teachers and not enough welders.

Indeed, there are few areas in which one could not find an example of something that did not work out the way it was supposed to. Medical planners, for instance, got the nation geared up for a massive effort to curtail a predicted swine flu epidemic that never came to pass. Yet at the same time the medical establishment was totally baffled by the completely unanticipated and mysterious "legionnaires' disease."

It was becoming apparent in the 1970s that the future was becoming harder and harder to keep under control, and there were growing pressures to plan and think further ahead. For one, technology itself was forcing people to begin thinking in terms that were fantastically long-range. In the 1950s tons of radioactive wastes from the nation's growing nuclear research effort were buried at the 600-square-mile Hanford Reservation in the state of Washington. Later, scientists realized that the site will not only be extremely dangerous for 400 years but will constitute enough of a health hazard for the next 50,000 years so that it will have to be guarded and kept off-limits, making the career of "nuclear guard" one with tremendous built-in job security. Then, there is the case of the Pioneer F spacecraft, launched by NASA in 1972, which is destined to be the first human-made object directed to escape from our solar system and make contact with beings in another. That spacecraft carries a small plaque containing a design intended to tell inhabitants of some other star system when and where it was launched and by what kind of creatures. The assumption made by those who designed and mounted the plaque was that if it is intercepted by others, it might not be for *millions of years.*

FUTURE SHOCK INTENSIFIED

All of these events and developments have served to strengthen the urge to get a better handle on future developments as individuals and institutions alike have come to feel the full impact of Alvin Toffler's term and book title, *Future Shock.* When that book came out in 1970, Toffler told us that we were being overwhelmed by the rate of change and speed of the future itself, an assessment which has proved to be one of the most on target of the 1970s.

If there was a turning point in all of this—a key moment at which the urge to cope with the future turned into a perceived need—it came in the form of the Arab oil boycott in October, 1973, which did for resources what Sputnik did for technology in 1957 and what Vietnam did to military planning. It was underscored again with the natural gas crisis which came during the cold winter of 1977. Although there are many examples of how these two crises were unanticipated and unplanned for, none is more dramatic than some lines which appeared in 1972 in the final report of the Presidential Commission on Population and the American Future. At one point the authors look far into the future and conclude, "With no major changes in technology, oil and gas supplies could become a problem for the United States by the year 2000—we would be importing more and paying higher prices: and supplies would be a problem for some world regions."

Within months it was clear that the year 2000 had arrived more than twenty-five years ahead of time.

There was more to it, however, than the fact that these crises were not predicted. Because both had to do with limited supplies, the crises brought about intensified interest in setting national goals, rational long-range planning, and conservation. What all sorts of institutions began to ask was how to anticipate and be prepared for future crises, shortages, and hard-to-predict events.

In the wake of the oil boycott, the gas shortage, and the possibility of more bad winters and deepening drought, many earlier visions of the future were being revised sharply. This is well illustrated by two *Wall Street Journal* articles on the future of food and agriculture published ten years apart. In 1966 the newspaper painted a bright picture which included the ability to produce up to 500 bushels of corn per acre "in the not too distant future" and the vision of farmers managing their fields from "towers containing television scanners to keep an eye on robot tractors." In 1976 the *Journal* published a "future revised" article which concluded that the prevention of starvation may become the world's number one concern by the year 2000 as food production falls off due to soaring energy costs and bad climate. All bets were off as experts were quoted as saying crop yields were plateau-ing and that corn production would probably not go far beyond the 1975 high of 116 bushels per acre—not 500. They said that automated farms would cost too much. In the 1966 article the talk was of "quite possibly cheaper food" in the year 2000. It is fact, not prediction, to say that food is going to cost substantially more in the year 2000. A number of factors had intervened between the two articles, the most important of which was 1966's widely held but wrong assumption that there was going to be an unlimited supply of cheap energy and good weather. Significantly, the 1976 article pointed out that the 1960s was an unusually good decade for weather with not one major crop failure due to climate. The *Journal* adds, "Weather historians quote the odds against such a decade [coming again] as 10,000 to 1."

THE FUTURE VS. FUTURISM

However, if the 1960s and 1970s are times in which the future itself has fared badly, futurism itself thrived and grew. This fact underscores the difference between the future and futurism, which are two entirely different things.

Before moving on to futurism, it is worthwhile to make a momentary report on the state of the present. Today's dilemmas have been stated in a number of ways, but few so succinctly and directly as a list of thirty issues formulated on the eve of the energy crisis (which would bring it to thirty-one) by Olaf Helmer, a noted futurist who became the nation's first full professor of futures research when he was appointed to that post at the University of Southern California in 1973.

1. The unsatisfactory condition of the economy
2. Foreign entanglements
3. Urban deterioration
4. Pollution
5. The crime rate
6. Inadequate housing
7. The drug problem
8. Poverty
9. Deficiencies in the educational system
10. Infringement of civil liberties
11. Inadequate health-care delivery
12. International antagonisms
13. The problem of the aged

14. Transportation and communication breakdown
15. Uncontrolled science and technology
16. The need for preservation of the environment
17. The difficulty of adjusting to changing value systems
18. Governmental disorganization
19. Race relations
20. Alienation from governmental processes
21. Deficiencies in the social security system
22. Institutional decay
23. The desire on the part of the young for radical change
24. Widespread anomie
25. The demand that corporations change their role in society
26. The population explosion
27. The impoverished cultural environment
28. The difficulties in overcoming sexual discrimination
29. Inadequate opportunities for self-fulfillmetnt
30. The deterioration of friendships and family ties

Basically, the Helmer list is not only a statement of the present predicament but a shopping list of issues that futurism must deal with. For the record, Helmer has written in a provocative paper, entitled "On the Future State of the Union," that in coming to grips with these issues we can expect major changes in the years ahead, including a severe drop in what he terms our "satisfaction indices." If that term sounds a bit abstract and dry, his specific accounting of those indices is not, for they are: personal physical security, economic prosperity, justice under the law, national security, social security, spiritual well-being, involvement of the individual in society, equality of opportunity, quality of the cultural environment, civil liberties, the quality of the technological environment, the quality of the physical environment, and the equitability of satisfaction. That is a powerful collection of things going into decline. Fortunately, Helmer's is but one of a variety of futures being painted for us.

3

THE FUTURISTS

You Can't Tell the Players
without a Taxonomy

Consider these statements about the future:

- This is the first age that's ever paid much attention to the future, which is a little ironic since we may not have one.

—Arthur C. Clarke

- I like the dreams of the future better than this history of the past.

—Thomas Jefferson, 1816
(from a letter to John Adams)

- The time has come for a dramatic reassessment of the directions of change, a reassessment made not by the politicians or the sociologists or the clergy or the elitist revolutionaries, not by technicians or college presidents, but by the people themselves. We need quite literally to "go to the people" with a question that is almost never asked of them: "What kind of a world do you want ten, twenty, or thirty years from now?" We need to initiate, in short, a continuing plebiscite on the future.

—Alvin Toffler, FUTURE SHOCK

These quotes represent *just a few* of many attitudes expressed about the future. For this reason, futurists spend inordinate amounts of time sorting and re-sorting individuals, groups, and visions of the future into categories.

Depending on who you talk to, all of contemporary

futurism is divided into two, three, four, five or more parts. It is enough to dazzle even behavioral scientists, who also seem prone to endless sorting and classifying.

Such systems or classifications—usually given the scientific title "taxonomy"—net charts and lists of attitudes and basic premises which are almost invariably complex and convoluted. But Roy Amara, a leading futures researcher who heads the Institute for the Future in Menlo Park, California, has worked up some taxonomies and come up with one which is both starkly simple and effective. He says there are three major boxes in which all of futurism fits: the analytical, visionary, and participatory—three that, in fact, respectively embrace the quotes from Clarke, Jefferson, and Toffler. Here then, using these boxes, are reports on what's current in all three future realms.

1. THE ANALYTICAL FUTURE

In 1973 a congressional committee wanted to get a reliable estimate on how much energy Americans would be using in 1980 and began collecting forecasts. When it finished, it had thirty-five different forecasts from nearly as many different sources. If that same committee were to go out for forecasts today for the year 1985, it would doubtlessly come back with a whole lot more . . . perhaps as many as a hundred or more of them and all from authoritative sources.

If this seems like an indictment of futurism, it is not meant to be. Instead it is meant to show the degree to which institutions are seriously attempting to get a grasp on the future and that a great deal of thought has gone into just one question about the future—albeit an important one. It is as much an indication of the fact that analytical futurism is still an imprecise endeavor as it is that it has arrived. Other things, such as the Futures Group's attraction for hundreds of clients, also attests to this.

Analytical futurism is, as the term makes clear, that form of the art in which likely futures are described and analyzed. It is meant to provide a framework which can be used for action, inaction, or adaptation. It is basically what the UN, CIA, Ford Motor Company, and you and I do when we think into the future. However, despite the precise ring to the word "analytical," different analyses of the same thing can yield very different results.

Undoubtedly the best-known and most current example of how analyses can differ is expressed by those whose work shows the world running out of everything (save for people and pollution) and those who have looked at the same data and concluded that we are in no such trouble and quite capable of solving our problems. The doomed view of earth has probably been most forcefully expressed by the futuristic Club of Rome and its famous computer-based *Limits to Growth* study, while the optimistic view has been most clearly expressed by the work of Herman Kahn and his Hudson Institute (and most particularly in his book *The Next 200 Years*). If you believe the Club of Rome's analysis, drastic action is called for, but if you believe Kahn, inaction seems appropriate.

The origins of this kind of futurism are twofold. The first has been the response to the growing uncertainty about the future coupled with intellectual push, which has come from a number of pioneering works, on the need for futures research. Although writers dating back to Voltaire and H. G. Wells have been discussing an art or science of futures research for a long time, it took the influence of a like-minded group of modern, articulate advocates to get the idea accepted. Among the most influential writings have been Bertand De Jouvenel's *Art of Conjecture*, John McHale's *Future of the Future*, and Dennis Gabor's *Inventing the Future*.

The other major influence has been the American military think tanks, which were created after World War II and given a number of jobs, including those of keeping an eye on the future of military technology and helping the armed services do their long-range planning. The most important of these outfits has been the RAND Corporation of Santa Monica, California, whose major support comes from the Air Force. Their work led to experimentation with new techniques for forecasting specific technical developments as well as with intellectual devices to help planners speculate about possible future military contingencies. Out of this came a basic package of methods for future thinking including scenario-writing, strategic games, mathematical models for predicting how a system might behave over time, and a procedure called "Delphi," which was created to get a consensus forecast on a specific future development from a panel of experts. (We'll look closely at these various methods in Chapter 4.) Not only were RAND and similar institutions like the Hudson Institute, Tempo, and the System Development Corporation coming up with a futurist methodology, but they were showing that this business of looking into the future had validity.

In some cases think-tank research yielded some remarkably accurate predictions, including such feats as picking the year of China's first nuclear detonation and the time of the first orbiting satellite by the Soviet Union. However, what was more important than these on-target forecasts was the bigger matter of helping their military clients look at alternative futures and the implications of each. The kind of future contingencies which were examined could be as basic—and chilling—as what are the possible ways in which a nuclear war can begin. A 1950s' inquiry into this particular issue by the RAND Corporation netted a number of conclusions, including the startling one that American nuclear warheads were especially vulnerable to an individual who wanted to set one off. This particular possibility horrified the military, which created safeguards to prevent it from happening.

A handful of companies and civilian agencies of government began to adapt some of these techniques to their operations, and academic interest in the subject of futurism continued to grow.

By the end of the 1960s futurism had attracted enough interest so that it could legitimately be called a significant intellectual movement with its own set of growing institutions. The scholarly journal *Futures* had come into being, the Institute for the Future opened its doors in 1968 as the first major futurist think tank, and the World Future Society was formed in 1966. Large international conferences were held on futures research in Oslo (1967) and Kyoto (1970), and major studies of the future were being commissioned by such no-nonsense organizations as the U.S. Office of Education, General Electric, and the American Academy of Arts and Sciences (with its well-known Commission on the Year 2000). By 1970 Norman Dalkey, a very influential RAND futurist, estimated that at least 400 independent research organizations in the United States alone were doing some sort of futures research.

What the 1970s have brought with them, insofar as analytical futurism is concerned, has been, basically, a lot more of the same. The proliferation includes not only courses, conferences, and publications but all sorts of new institutions. Futuristic consulting firms like the Futures Group, Applied Futures Inc., and Forecasting International Ltd. came into being, as did a number of nonprofit think tanks and foundations with names like the Committee for the Future, Worldwatch Institute, Futuremics, and the Center for Futures Research.

The Government Futurists

But if there is one major piece of news in all of this, it is that in the last few years futurism has gained a significant foothold at the highest levels of industry and government. Today nobody can say, as one could just a few years ago, that futurism is primarily contained in closed loops of experts, futures buffs, think-tank types, and intellectuals.

The evidence is most dramatic at the highest levels of government. Shortly before taking office, President Carter pledged that he would "press every government agency to pursue futures research" and attempt to involve the public in these activities. Carter's past involvement with long-range planning and futurism dates back to his experience in developing the Polaris program—a project which is still considered a prime example of effective long-range planning and scheduling. While he was governor of Georgia, he launched a major project for setting future goals for the state, complete with citizen involvement and a planning unit within the state government. One result of this process was the establishment of the first state "Heritage Trust," which is a permanent mechanism for the preservation of historic and ecologically important sites in the state. However, probably the best example of the man's ability to plan and shape the future may have been expressed in his carefully calculated twenty-two-month rise from relative obscurity to his election as President. Carter's acid test as a futurist may come with his energy plan, which incorporates the most important attributes of contemporary futurism, in that it is long-term, multidisciplinary, and aimed at developing an acceptable alternative.

For its part, Congress has adopted a sudden and impressive concern for futurism, which has included the formation of a futures research unit in the Library of Congress, an internal Congressional Clearinghouse on the Future, several symposia and hearings on futurism, and a potentially important 1975 House rule which states that every congressional committee ". . . shall on a continuing basis undertake future research and forecasting on matters within the jurisdiction of that committee." This futures rule is beginning to be used, as are hearings held to look at future goals and realities in different areas. As they begin, there has been the stunning realization that in one area after another the United States does its official business by reacting to "oversight" rather than "foresight." When hearings began on the future of American foreign policy, its chairman noted that this was the first occasion since World War II that the nation was to take a comprehensive look at its present and future position in the world.

This congressional fascination with the future does not appear to be a mere fad but rather a genuine attempt to come to grips with its own past inability to think ahead. Many members share the feeling of Senator Abraham Ribicoff who said recently, "Usually government acts on facts and theories that are already out of existence. So in 1976, we are really attempting to solve the problems of 1971 instead of the problems of 1981." A case in point has been Congress's inability to catch up with the computer age. Only recently has Congress set up a committee to look at its own future use of computers, a move that was occasioned by the continuing embarrassment of fact-finding committees not having information on key issues. Representative Charlie Rose of North Carolina, a declared futurist and the chairman for the new computer committee, has pointed out that other institutions are "light-years ahead" of Congress in handling information on energy and other key issues. He says that when their interests are at stake "the multinational corporations, the financial institutions, and the other giants of business most often know the answers before Congress has had a chance to formulate the questions."

Foresight

All of this legislative interest in the future shows signs of even further growth, as ideas which are now only being proposed come into being. There are a number of them, including Senator Edward Kennedy's call for the creation of an "Experimental Futures Agency" which would build "showcase" communities and institutions using the newest technology. Meanwhile, the Senate is currently considering several options which would give it the equivalent of the House's foresight provision. The futures research unit in the Library of Congress is establishing a computerized system for future-oriented information called FIRST (for Futures Information Retrieval System).

Although they are not always labeled with the word "future" in the title, Congress has also made or is working on other future-oriented moves. The most important has to be the Congressional Office of Technology Assessment (OTA), which began operating in 1974 under the direction of former Representative Emilio Q. Daddario of Connecticut, who was the man who had first begun to push for the idea in Congress in the 1960s. The OTA basically serves as a technological early warning system which addresses itself to the potential consequences, both positive and negative, of new technology. During its short existence it has probed into a number of things, including matters as diverse as the consequences of stepped-up oil and gas exploration, options available in making oil tanker operations safer and less prone to polluting the oceans, and new means for understanding the dynamics of auto collisions.

(One option which is under investigation is the development of crash recorders, like the famous black boxes now installed in all commercial airliners, for cars.)

Dennis Little, who heads the futures research unit in the Library of Congress, sums up what is going on: "There is now a significant and growing hard-core group of members and staff people who are intensely serious about futures research. As simple as it sounds, these people realize that history is important but the only thing they can do anything about is the future."

Bureaucratic Futures

This new future fascination is also showing itself in other parts of government too. A decade ago the lion's share of research of this type in the federal agencies was confined to the military, which was (and still is) working up forecasts of new technology starting with such efforts as the Air Force's massive (fourteen-volume) and secret "Operation Forecast." Today examples abound all over government. The military itself has stopped merely trying to forecast new technology and is now looking at such diverse matters as long-range petroleum availability and the future of Chinese military power. The Army is actually working on a computer model which will be able to assess the racial climate in military units in order to predict those which are most likely to erupt in racial crises. Elsewhere one can find work in progress on such pieces of the future puzzle as the role of cmmunications in the cities of the future (Housing and Urban Development), alternative future automobile fuels (the Environmental Protection Agency), projections on the future age composition of the American population (Housing and Urban Development), the future research role of the universities (the Office of Education), energy options for New York City (the National Science Foundation), the future of the soybean (Agriculture), and even one called "Forecasts of Future Household Solid Waste Generation" from the Environmental Protection Agency.

It is one thing to commission a few studies on the future and quite another to make a deeper commitment to futures research. More and more agencies are making that leap by creating permanent internal futures research and forecasting groups in addition to one-shot study efforts. The Federal Aviation Agency, U.S. Patent Office, Army, Environmental Protection Agency, Energy Research and Development Agency, and the Department of Agriculture are among those which have created such units.

Elsewhere in the world, national interest in futurism in some countries has equaled, or even excelled, that being expressed in the United States. Sweden actually formed a Secretariat for Future Studies in 1972, and futures research has become especially important in France, the Netherlands, Japan, and the Soviet Union. Wayne Boucher, a researcher who has been working on a major study of the field for the National Science Foundation, says, "One thing I've learned from this study is that Soviet work in the field is much more extensive than had been previously thought."

Industry Futurists

In the private sector, scores of companies both in the United States and abroad now have single futurists or futures groups on their payrolls. Organizations which have made this commitment to the future include Shell Oil, Volvo, General Mills, Monsanto, General Electric, Uniroyal, Gillette, Whirlpool, and Western Electric. These groups differ from traditional planning groups in that they look beyond the normal five- to ten-year planning period. Thaddeus Obal of the long-range analysis group at the Mobil Oil Corporation explains what long-range means in this context: "[Our] time horizon has been out to the year 2000, and in some cases to the year 2020. The reasons are fairly obvious. The energy industry in general is subject to long lead times. Some energy problems don't become critical until fifteen or twenty years out. On the other hand, some current energy problems are related to physical, technological, political and economic restraints that may prevent any meaningful solution within a ten-year period."

Normally these groups do not map out a company's corporate strategy but rather point to potential opportunities and problems down the road. Typically, they are as much concerned with forthcoming technical developments and the availability of raw materials as they are with social and economic trends. Understandably, there is a limit to the information which comes out of these groups, for obvious competitive reasons. However, as more and more information gets out on how some of the pioneers in the field use their information, the more apparent it becomes that futurism can be extremely useful in business. One example which was reported in an 1975 *Wall Street Journal* article tells of a forecasting effort at Whirlpool in the early 1960s that correctly spotted the coming of permanent-press fabrics. That forecast enabled the company to be the first on the market with washers and dryers with special settings for those fabrics. The example is prosaic when compared to the anticipation of major social and scientific developments, but it is just the kind of thing that gives one company an edge over another.

In some cases corporate futurism has become a very ambitious activity. One such example is the Business Planning Group of Bell Canada in Montreal. This group is not only involved in a variety of futures research activities but has also created a special future-oriented "environment" which may be truly unique. This environment, which was created to give the company's planning group special freedom and flexibility, is looked upon as a futuristic experiment of its own—perhaps a prototype of the white-collar work place of the future. The environment includes an electronic futures information system so that forecasts can be found quickly, and a "paperless office" concept, in which a highly sophisticated package of equipment has turned many routine operations into high-speed electronic functions. Most "paperwork" appears in the form of illuminated text on the screens of video terminals. Memos and messages are sent electronically, and reports are edited right on the screen. Some terminals are portable, which allows members of the group to plug into the office—or electronically commute—and work from their homes or from other cities.

Meanwhile, the final and perhaps most influential forces in analytical futurism are the futures think tanks. Here is a profile of one of the most important.

The Futures Group

It is located in a low-rise office complex in the tidy but lackluster Hartford suburb of Glastonbury, Connecticut. If one somehow expects the innards of a very important futures consulting firm to look or feel different than the spaces occupied by a group of accountants or claims adjusters, they are wrong.

There are no data terminals on the desks, nor any of that atrocious computer-generated "art"—let alone anything more sophisticated. The first words you hear are not of industrial robots or anomalies in the pattern of basic social indicators, but a woman talking about her new diet. The first things your eyes focus on: some yellowing cartoons taped to the bulletin board, a few leggy unbionic plants, and a half-eaten doughnut in one of the cubbyholes in which the Futures Group's mail is sorted.

Appearances are deceiving, however, because a number of institutional clients have beaten a path to this same door in order to get a bead on some aspect of the future. Since it was founded in 1971 with an initial staff of four, the size of the group has grown to about fifty. It has studied all sorts of things—all, that is, starting with "the future of"— including: legalized gambling, livestock, the human consumption of fats and oils, the scientific journal, prepaid legal services, the U.S. Postal Service, shipping, travel, biological research, leisure, the U.S. economy, and plastics.

In the few years since it has opened it has worked for more than 500 clients, which are almost all institutions: United States and foreign government agencies, trade associations, foundations, and private companies. In many cases the actual name of the client it is working for is listed as "proprietary" (even in the booklet that brags about some of the big jobs it has done). In a number of examples the clients are further identified but with nothing more than a weak clue, such as "a large multinational corporation," a "pharmaceutical manufacturer," or a "major utility." In the course of a conversation with officials of the Futures Group you are told of a study that was completed for an unspecified federal agency on a "proprietary" basis. One need not be an expert in the ways of government to guess the name of (better yet, the initials of) the agency in question. However, the clients whose identities are known indicate that the group works primarily for entities with clout: NASA, Harvard, the Electronics Industry Association, the state of Texas, and the National Science Foundation.

The Prophet/Profit Motive

The bulk of the work of the Futures Group goes into formal studies which address themselves to some specific aspect of the future. Most of these are done for one client and are often both extensive and expensive. A major assessment of "life-extending" technologies (pacemakers, dialysis machines, etc.) being conducted at the time of my visit was being financed through a contract with the National Science Foundation for $294,933. It also does certain studies of broader interest, such as one recent look at the future of government and industry relations in America, which are distributed to those willing to pay for a copy. These studies are usually priced in the range of $3,000 to $4,000 a copy.

Studies tend to differ considerably, so it would be inaccurate to talk about a typical one. However, a five-volume study completed by the Group for the California Energy Resources Conservation and Development Commission shows the span of futures-related work a single study is likely to encompass. Each section addresses itself to some aspect of the future of energy and gas in the state, ranging from a volume on "Methodology and Research Needs" to one which summarizes scores of interviews with dozens of experts on the energy prospects in the state. Most interesting, however, is the first volume, which looks at many factors, some ostensibly unrelated to energy, and forecasts and summarizes them in an attempt to give energy policy-makers an idea of the forces that will shape future demands. These include the size of labor force, recreation use, and other factors which ultimately have an impact on energy.

To give an idea of how specific the report is, the forecast for the California labor force begins by stating that it will grow because of two factors: the increase in the middle-aged population and substantial increases in the numbers of working women. ("Even a rise in birthrate will not necessarily cause a slowing of the trend," says the report.) However, the outlook changes thereafter:

By 1990, a sharp drop in the 20–40 year age group will occur, significantly reducing the number of new entrants to the labor force. Consequently, a labor shortage is likely during the 1990–1995 time period, which may mark a resurgence in labor migration to California (1990–1995 will coincide with a period of very large world population in the 20–40 year age group). About this time, the steady growing population of elderly will begin an even steeper rise. And many senior citizens may seek second careers and avocations due to discontent (with unproductive life-styles) and ever-rising costs of living.

Further along, the areas of concern and the forecasts become more and more specific, to the point where comparative projections are made for fishing, water skiing, snow skiing, and other leisure activities in California in 1990. By that year Californians and visitors to the state will spend 111 million days fishing, which is an increase of 74 percent from 1970 (just nosing out water skiing, which will increase 73 percent during the same period). Snow skiing will make the largest percentage jump (up 82 percent), but it will still only account for less than 1 percent of the recreational demand.

Besides researching a specific subject for a fee, the group provides a number of other services ranging from relatively informal ones like addressing a corporation's top brass on future planning to its data services which are called PROSPECTS and SCOUT (both ®). PROSPECTS is a service tailored to individual industries which offers clients some remarkably specific forecasts made by the Futures

Group, while SCOUT is a collection of forecasts made mostly by others. The first series of PROSPECTS forecasts, which has been prepared for the drug industry, addresses itself to such detailed year-by-year forecasts as the average cost of a prescription, the number of new drug applications accepted by the Food and Drug Administration, and sales of tranquilizers. SCOUT, on the other hand, may be the closest thing our technical, information-rich society has to the oracles of antiquity. It is a computerized data bank which has been fed tens of thousands of forecasts on virtually every topic imaginable. A client wishing to zero in on the subject of leisure can get a SCOUT print-out on that subject containing hundreds of specific forecasts. SCOUT searches cost between $975 and $1,950.

Hal Becker, vice-president and treasurer of the Futures Group, is a futurist who does not like that term. He thinks the title has an aura that sounds both presumptuous and science-fictionlike. "What we do here," he says, "is policy analysis. We work with our clients in order to help them try to come up with the best decisions in the face of an uncertain future. We are not looking at a single future but at a variety of them and offering to help people get ready for them."

Becker candidly points out that the early success of the group may have had less to do with the group itself than with events, specifically the Arab oil boycott. "Many of our clients are extremely interested in learning to see those events which might point to another boycott—to minimize shock and surprise."

The Futures Group is a prime example of one of the new institutions that have cropped up in recent years to help make the transition from today to tomorrow and attempt to minimize institutional future shock. While it is an important example, it is hardly the only one of this size and scope. The nonprofit Institute for the Future, the World Future Society, the Hudson Institute, and the Center for the Study of Social Policy at the Stanford Research Institute are just a few other futures think tanks now in operation. The Yellow Pages in Part II of this book list some more.

2. THE VISIONARY FUTURE

Hazel Henderson, co-director of the Princeton Center for Alternative Futures, told a recent congressional seminar on the future that her candidate for "the best U.S. futurism of the past five years" was *The Whole Earth Catalog*.

While other analytical futurists might disagree with that choice, it drives home the generally undisputed point that some of the most important "futurists" are people like Steward Brand, prime organizer of *The Whole Earth Catalog*, who do not call themselves futurists and are not normally invited to the big powwows on the year 2000. Henderson and other proclaimed futurists also make the case that if one were making a list of important futurists of this type it would have to include such people as Ralph Nader, Margaret Mead, Rachel Carson, and Martin Luther King, Jr.

Although this aspect of futurism is extremely important, it is also extremely difficult to pin down. It is hard to define except in the most general terms (roughly, that which advances and/or advocates an image of the future which is counter to conventional expectations) and even harder to sort out in terms of which visions are important and which are trivial. A new and influential vision is almost impossible to predict in advance for the simple reason that it is a new vision. It becomes predictable only at the moment at which it is first accepted and even then its long-term importance is not always clear. Moreover, such visions are not governed by a set of rules; for instance, they do not have to be future-oriented to have an influence on the future (as may well prove to be the case with Alex Haley's *Roots*) and can, in fact, fail most miserably when they are precisely aimed at the future (such as has been the case with a number of already forgotten attempts to stir up new visions for the United States during the Bicentennial).

There are a number of current examples of those advancing new visions, ranging from individuals to several movements that have actually grown to the point where they represent fairly sizable subcultures. One of these is represented by those working under the umbrella term of "unconventional science" (bioenergetics, parasensory phenomena, Kirlian electrophotography, cryonics, etc.) and another by those who practice and advocate "appropriate" or "soft" technology—the low-energy, nonpolluting alternative to high technology. Another is the peace research movement, which has as its central premise the belief that the war disease can be cured. It is something worth examining as an example of a visionary future.

Thinking Peace

Putting the study of peace on a footing as secure as that long provided for war and weapons research is hardly a new idea, but it was not until the last decade that the effort to mobilize brainpower to create and maintain peace gained any real ground. With little fanfare a small but ever-widening circle of scholars has launched numerous peace research projects and issued calls for even grander schemes—for instance, asking for a massive international crash program against the causes of war, to be mounted with the same sense of urgency that attended the Manhattan Project.

These researchers have started councils, study groups, institutes and journals, and read footnote-laden papers to each other at international forums. Their research menu has been rich and varied: the dynamics of national decision-making, the art of bargaining in a time of crisis, gaming situations aimed at finding keys to conflict resolution, the applicability of nonmilitary (or nonviolent) national defense, the technology of policing weapons bans, social indicators of impending conflict, and many others. Such efforts have attracted people ranging from legal scholars, who have plunged into the fine print of long-ago broken treaties to see why they soured, to determined data collectors, who have fed information on past wars into their computers to try to uncover clues to the patterns which lead to war (with such work yielding curious bits of information like the fact that April and October are the two months in which a war is most likely to get underway).

During the same period the idea of researching peace

has looked more and more like an absolute necessity than a scholarly whim—and perhaps more absurd as well, in the face of what this decade is bringing. Arms spending has jumped by two thirds from the previous decade to a level of over $200 billion a year, a sum which matches the total yearly income of all the developing nations of the earth combined. Worldwide military research and development have reached the level at which they effectively tie up about one quarter of all scientists and engineers. In the nuclear realm, the term "overkill" has become something of a quaint bit of 1955ish understatement, as the thermonuclear arsenal now provides a punch equal to tens of TNT per head of human stock. Meanwhile, the range, speed, and what-have-you of all those conventional items that go WHIZ-SWISH-BANG have improved considerably. Wars have raged here and there while the meetings went on. By one recent count, U.S. and Soviet negotiators had met officially almost 6,000 times since 1945 to discuss arms limitations of one sort or another.

Trying to break this pattern, the United Nations proclaimed the 1970s the Disarmament Decade, during which the program for complete general disarmament would be framed. With the decade mostly spent, the situation is worse, not better.

Given this state of affairs, it is not surprising that so many are increasingly being attracted to peace research, particularly since the name has such a nice, idealistic ring. Just as military strategists with their missile studies and pacification plans have been known to call themselves peace researchers, so too have radical analysts who presuppose that the only way to achieve a peaceful world is to uncork the conflicts and revolutions that will destroy the institutions that inhibit peace. The appeal of peace research is such that the United Nations General Assembly resolved a few years ago that peace research is a good thing and should be pursued; it is beginning to attract smart foundation money, and all sorts of scholarly and scientific associations are tacking "Peace Research and Conflict Resolution" sessions onto the agendas of their annual meetings. Most important, peace research and its natural ally peace education are beginning to boom in the United States, taking the lead from northern Europe, where such things are already quite popular and continue to bloom.

The reason that peace research began to gather idealistic, antiwar, and pacifist-oriented scholars in the 1960s was that it was seen as both a rejection of the world created by the Cold War politicians who had led the world to the nuclear brink and an affirmation of their own desire to match personal ideology to their work. Though it drew its strength from moral indignation, anxiety, and emotion, its general premise was that peace had to be put on a sounder, more scientific footing than traditional morality, placards, and good intentions. The working imperative of nascent peace research was that the conditions of war, peace, and conflict had to be understood and that, once understood, war could be attacked on the same basis as that used to attack disease. The generally acknowledged but vague intention was applied science which, like medicine, would draw on existing sciences and disciplines.

From the outset, the research was to be international in its outlook and a rejection of the kind of nationalistic research pursued by such government-supported think tanks as the RAND Corporation in the United States, which was chartered to promote the security of the country. The peace researcher was not to be confused with the strategists who, in the words of Bert V. A. Roling, former head of the International Peace Research Association, ". . . want to ensure peace by 'deterrence' by 'the balance of terror,' the modern interpretations of the ancient adage: *si vis pacem para bellum*—if you wish for peace prepare for war."

The fact was that while there were only a few small institutes in the world completely devoted to the subject in 1960, by 1970 the total had jumped to scores of full-fledged peace research institutes along with a host of attendant phenomena ranging from departments of "peace research" or "conflict resolution" at several universities to two active international associations. This growth indicates the extent of peace research. Today the number has risen significantly both in the world at large and in the United States, where the movement seemed to be slower in getting started. The Consortium on Peace Research, Education and Development (COPRED), which was founded in 1970 as an umbrella organization for American efforts, now has more than 100 institutions associated with it, ranging from organizations like the World Law Fund to the Center for Peaceful Change, which came into being at Kent State University in 1971 as a living memorial to the four students who were slain there in 1970. University-level peace studies programs have proliferated to the point that the Center for Peace Studies at the University of Akron now publishes the *International Peace Studies Newsletter*.

Currently the efforts that are going on in the field of peace research and education are diverse. Here is just a small sampling.

• At the Canadian Peace Research Institute in Oakville, Ontario, work is in progress on a major study called the "Limits to Violence" project, which is a model that parallels the Club of Rome's *Limits to Growth* study. The Canadian model examines three kinds of violence—domestic, international, and structural (or that which stems from inequality between and within nations, such as death from malnutrition)—in an effort to establish leads to their causes. Although the project was only partially completed when this was written, some early conclusions have been made on the nature of violence by Norman Alcock, who is running the project. For example, one new "law" which can be stated from the research into structural violence is that for every 7.7 percent increase in GNP per capita in a nation, life expectancy goes up exactly one year until GNP reaches $600 per capita. To continue, quoting from the interim report, "But from $1,000 per year per capita on through to the richest nation, life expectancy is almost independent of wealth." After $1,000 the political regime takes over as the determinant: people in the democratic socialist nations live longer than those in either the communist or democratic capitalist nations.

• A nonpartisan, public interest effort based in Washington is lobbying to get the nation to establish a National Academy of Peace, which would be sort of a West Point for the nonmilitary resolution of conflict. Those behind this effort, which is called the National Peace Academy Campaign, see a number of signs which indicate that their goal is an attainable one—despite the fact that more than 140 bills have been introduced in Congress to set up an academy or department of peace since 1935. (The idea is actually not new to America, since George Washington recommended "a proper peace establishment" back in 1782.)

• In 1966 when the Swedes decided to mark the fact that their nation had enjoyed 150 years of unbroken peace, they rejected the idea of a marble monument or some other inanimate object and instead created an independent peace research institute with an international staff. Today the Stockholm International Peace Research Institute (SIPRI) is a small but highly respected one-of-a-kind outfit which is attempting to positively affect arms control and disarmament by revealing all that it can to the world on the continuing weapons spiral. The role it has chosen for itself is that of an international conscience trying to defuse the world by revealing cold facts and calling bluffs. SIPRI's disarming audacity is best shown in its *Yearbooks*, which are thick report cards that annually detail major changes in the world's arsenals and national military postures. It constantly delivers carefully documented messages to the world, some of which are having an impact. (Sample: No matter what weapons freezes come out of the SALT agreements, the nuclear arms race will continue, albeit in a new direction, unless military research and development are curtailed.) SIPRI has been instrumental in sounding the bell on the dangers of nuclear power plants which will create a plutonium supply sufficient to produce 100 Hiroshima-sized bombs a week by 1980. The significance of SIPRI today is that it has the resources and reputation needed to keep the world alert to the realities of arms and disarmament by delivering steady doses of truthful, timely, and pertinent information.

• The Institute for World Order in New York has been working for several years with international teams of peace researchers to construct models for the world in the year

2000 in which peace, social justice, economic well-being, and ecological balance prevail. Now the Institute is working on its "Lodi Project," which is an attempt to create a single composite model based on the earlier collection of models. If this all sounds a bit too ivory-towerish, the Institute is also working on political strategies for the 1980–1985 period to help it get its model adopted. This effort is being funded by the Rockefeller Foundation and the Carnegie Endowment for International Peace, among others.

However encouraging this is, the scholarly hunt for the elusive dynamics of peace is of course fraught with countless risks and pitfalls (not the least of which are unhealable schisms between groups, faddism, the problem of being totally ignored, and the threat of being used as adjuncts to strategic military thinking). It is also patently absurd—for how else could you term a growing but underfunded network of academics and activists who have decided to try to bring about a peaceful world? Yet although it is easy to look upon these efforts skeptically and dismiss them, historically, visionaries have had a way of beating the odds and gaining prominence when they are least expected to.

3. THE PARTICIPATORY FUTURE

Alvin Toffler of *Future Shock* fame not only gave the process its name but has become its tireless chief advocate: the name is "Anticipatory Democracy" and the process is basically that of involving great numbers of people in future planning. Toffler maintains that we have become a nation of increasingly angry "plannees" whose future is being managed for us by the big institutions of government, labor, business, and science. In order to turn plannees into planners, Toffler has formed a loose confederation called the A/D Network which is made up of people who agree on the need for the process and believe that in order to have an Anticipatory Democracy there are two things which must happen. The first is expanding the "future-consciousness" of all segments of the public and the second is to get people participating in the planning process at all levels.

While the network itself is conspicuously lacking in organization (no funds, no membership lists—not even a permanent address), it is showing a remarkable ability to attract attention and apostles, ranging from Buckminster Fuller and Betty Friedan to a growing number of members of Congress. In fact, one of the places where Toffler's process is being most discussed is in Congress. In 1975, some thirty members held a well-attended conference on Anticipatory Democracy during which Toffler and other social critics talked about Congress's need to get in touch both with the future and with the people of the United States. Since then Toffler has made several other appearances on Capitol Hill, during which he chided his hosts for their inflexibility and old-fashioned ways. For example, early in 1977 he addressed a dinner set up by the Congressional Clearinghouse on the Future, during which he said in part, "The committee structure is outmoded. The world is simply not chopped up in nice little pieces like it is cut up by committee jurisdictions." He then went on to point out that the futures of, say, agriculture and foreign policy are definitely intertwined. He actually suggested that farmers be asked to testify at foreign relations hearings to get their advice on what was important.

There is much indication that the A/D process is gaining momentum in various parts of the country. There have been a series of major projects which attempt to combine future consciousness with grass roots planning. It is not really clear whether or not the A/D Network has been directly responsible for this, or whether it is simply an expression of an idea whose time has come. It is probably a combination of both.

The Next Minnesota?

In January, 1977, the participatory Commission on Minnesota's Future came out with a plan for the future of the state in the form of a slick, well-written, eighty-three-page report. It opens with talk of great promise for the state but also of inevitable hardships, shortages, rising prices, and an end to the ever-rising standard of living. After making some general points it goes on to make dozens of specific recommendations and suggested approaches for the future.

What is interesting about the plan is not its general concept, which adheres to well-meaning but fuzzy principles common to most plans, but the specific ideas that it promotes. While a few of these ideas are startling in and of themselves, it is their collective impact that is startling, for after you have gone through them, it is apparent that if a majority are carried out, the next Minnesota will be a lot different from the present one. Here is an abbreviated sampling of those suggestions:

• Eliminate all local zoning ordinances and construction codes and establish statewide standards.
• Consider creating a new form of state government: such as a one-house legislature or a parliamentary state with a "first minister" elected by the parliament instead of a governor.
• Actively encourage a future for the small, family-owned farm.
• Offer state subsidies for building insulation and give tax incentives for people who drive "energy-efficient" cars.
• Start up a broad plan to encourage lifelong learning which would include such things as educational sabbaticals for all employed people, schools that are open all year long, earlier and more flexible retirement, and the common use of colleges and universities by older adults.
• Encourage large and small solar energy installations in the state and explore new energy concepts such as district heating plants and peat gasification.
• Enact a broad series of programs and regulations to foster the maintenance, rehabilitation, and remodeling of existing housing throughout the state.
• Mount a major effort to bring rising medical costs under control through preventive care, paraprofessionals, telecommunications networks, and noninstitutional care (such as encouraging families to care for members who would normally be put in a nursing home or mental hospital).

The commission that prepared the report was one created in 1973 by the governor and legislature. In the course of coming up with its package of recommendations, it worked with citizens groups, farm and labor organizations, businesses, and agencies of both the state and federal governments. Though it has attracted little national attention, the commission's work has been well publicized within Minnesota through regional public meetings and live radio and television coverage of its hearings on the future of the state. Now only time will tell how and to what degree the future envisioned by the report will become a reality.

The "Tomorrow/2000/Goals" Boom— Grass Roots Futurism

The Minnesota plan is just one example of a growing urge by states and local communities to create special groups to plan their futures in the spirit of Anticipatory Democracy. Some are public, some private, some permanent, and some temporary, but they all have certain basic traits in common: the desire to come up with a working long-range plan, the involvement of citizens in the planning process, and a position outside the local bureaucracy. The movement began in the early 1960s with the California Tomorrow plan and grew significantly in the 1970s as groups like Goals for Georgia, the Hawaii Commission on the Year 2000, the Commission on Maine's Future, Vermont Tomorrow, Alternatives for Washington, Florida 2000, the Oregon Tomorrow Foundation, and Massachusetts Tomorrow came into being. In addition, a number of more localized groups, like Seattle 2000, Hoosier 2000 (Columbus, Indiana), and Austin Tomorrow, have come into being in places as small as Clarinda, Iowa, with a population of 5,500. (Not to laugh—the goals group in Clarinda has a budget, $20,000, that is the same as that for the statewide Iowa project.) Going in the other direction, several regional groups like Great Lakes Tomorrow, Inc., and the Commission on the Future of the South have been created.

All of these efforts have gotten lumped together into what the Futures Research Group at the Library of Congress has dubbed "the Tomorrow/2000/Goals" movement. It is hard to go too far in generalizing about the movement as a whole because the groups operate so differently, but it is instructive to look at some of the things they are doing or have done.

While all of the groups rely on citizen participation, the means of getting people involved differs significantly. In Vermont, for example, questionnaires on the future of the state were distributed on March 1, 1977, at town meetings which were held throughout the state on that day. The Iowa 2000 effort was touched off with an "Iowa Quiz" which appeared in all of the state's Sunday newspapers asking what kind of future the people wanted for the state. Sample returns from the quiz were tabulated and analyzed on a one-hour television special, hosted by Harry Reasoner, which was shown on all sixteen stations in the state. Others have used statewide opinion polls, marathon public brainstorming sessions, "Futures Carnivals," local and regional planning conferences, speakers bureaus, student assemblies, and newsletters.

In some cases the approaches take on futuristic aspects of their own. One important element of Santa Barbara's future-oriented ACCESS program (for Alternative Comprehensive Environmental Study System) is a Situation Room, which has been described as a combination of a never-ending New England town meeting (to which citizens come to express their concerns about the future) and an electronic Command and Control center for keeping tabs on information. The room contains such specific equipment as an electronic polling system, a computer-assisted visual display board, and a hookup which allows it to plug into cable television stations.

Californias One and Two

Different vehicles are used to get people to think about the future. The ground-breaking California Tomorrow program, a private group with 4,500 members who are trying to get the state to adopt a comprehensive plan for the future, came up with an interesting device for making its point: detailed descriptions of three Californias. California

Zero is the present state, California One projects present trends and ways of dealing with problems into a rather dismal future, and California Two is ". . . a proposal for the alternative way of solving problems; an outline of what government and private enterprise would have to do to carry out this alternative and a view of what life might be like in California Two." The device is especially graphic when California One and Two are compared on their specifics. For example, here is a glimpse of the future of transportation in California One:

By 1999 there are 23 million automobiles in California. Traffic congestion increases even with additional freeways. Downtown centers have grown inaccessible as they have grown tall. They depend heavily on access by the automobile, but there is paralyzing local street congestion and parking is expensive and inadequate. Existing freeways have been widened or added to, up to quadruple decking. Inner-city populations still lack convenient access to many areas, both within and outside the cities.

The picture in California Two, however, looks like this:

Public transportation forms the skeleton of entire urban regions. Regional transportation systems are based on a combination of rapid transit lines of various kinds—mini-rail, computer-controlled jitneys, buses, other feeder vehicles, and "people moving" conveyances in commercial centers or neighborhood residential areas. Nonpolluting autombiles are used extensively, but it is not necessary for individuals to own automobiles; there are attractive alternatives . . .

In addition to descriptions, there are cost estimates for various elements of the two Californias which attempt to show that Two can live as cheaply as One. To continue the transportation theme, here is how the plan estimates future costs (in 1970 dollars) through the year 2000.

Item	California One	California Two
Transit system installation	$ 2.5 billion	$ 6.5 billion
Freeway construction	$ 8.0 billion	$ 4.0 billion
Total	$10.5 billion	$10.5 billion

There is also an estimate of the annual operating costs of the two systems by 2000 in which California Two's transportation system actually costs less to run. It only works out this way, however, if you count the costs of such things as air pollution, lost travel time, and parking lot maintenance.

Televised Town Meeting

Another vehicle which groups use to foster thinking and decision-making about the future are one-shot events used to heighten future consciousness. Massachusetts' 1976 "Town Meeting of the Future" was such an event. It was co-sponsored by the Massachusetts Bicentennial Commission, the World Future Society, and WGBH-TV and produced by Interobang Ideas, a small group which specializes in staging futuristic events. The meeting was an all-televised, two-day affair involving some 275 experts, decision-makers, and informed citizens whose job it was to come up with an agenda for the future for the Commonwealth's 351 cities and towns. In the final session fifteen "Warrant Articles" were presented and voted on by the participants. Many of the articles contained the predictable generalized suggestions (preservation of the competitive free-market economy, curtailing wasteful consumption, tax reform, preservation of ecological diversity, and so forth) that tend to come out of such forums. However, there were two articles, both specific attempts to insure greater citizen control, which received the unanimous approval of those voting. The final versions of these two articles read as follows.

Article 8: *Social Needs and Government*

To overcome the growing sense of distrust of people and institutions which attends social complexity, we need to promote increased individual and community participation in the making of decisions which affect our collective future.

By opening essential procedures of government, such as policy-making and program-budgeting, to citizen decision.

By establishing area councils for citizen consideration and direction of governmental policies, programs, and any other matters affecting the lives of citizens.

By creating a network of citizen-controlled information centers—established as intermediaries between the citizenry and community or government agencies —to receive information from the government; to assemble and disseminate this information to users of services, to information-gathering agencies, and to the media; to serve, also, as ombudsman toward openness of government, citizen input and two-way accessibility of information.

ARTICLE 14: *Information Evolution and Applied Technology*

Establish local "Committees of Communication" to study citizen informational needs for personal and public planning.

Establish a state "Resource Network" to give citizens access to global data, expertise, two-way media, and action alliances.

Not all ideas were as well received. One that was "strongly" defeated had to do with the future of art in the state.

ARTICLE 5: *Art and Human Nature in Evolution*

To seek a revitalization of traditional systems by asking the cities and towns of the United States to consider requiring each community to create anew cultural objects and events public places every five years and to make art-as-property illegal.

Massachusetts, by the way, may lay claim to the title of the state with the strongest attempts to get control of its future. There is the private Massachusetts Tomorrow group, which is basically run by a corps of 500 volunteers who are working on "value questions" for the future. There's a Special Legislative Commission on Growth and the Quality of Life. One of the most important results of the commission's activities has been the passage of the state's Growth Policy Development Act, which provides for local committees, made up of officials and citizens, helping to plan the statewide process. To date, more than 90 percent of the Commonwealth's municipalities have joined in the effort to plan from the "bottom up."

Future Problems?

Of course, there are some who are not at all sure that the process of A/D will work out as ideally as Toffler and so many others now suggest. Futurist Daniel Bell actually goes so far as to warn that he thinks that participation will ultimately increase personal frustration with government. He has written in his book, *The Coming of Post-Industrial Society*, "The expansion of the political arena and the involvement of a greater number of persons simply means that it takes more time, and more cost, to reach a decision and to get anything done."

While Bell worries about what will happen if these participatory schemes are taken seriously, there is perhaps even more future frustration if all of this good "citizen input" is disregarded. For example, a number of these groups are asking rather straightforward questions, like this one taken from an actual statewide poll:

Much of the commercial development in Vermont has taken the form of shopping malls and shopping centers. Many people welcome the malls because they are convenient and have a diversity of shopping opportunities. Others claim they are eyesores and decrease the viltality of town or village centers. In considering the future commercial development, should public officials ("X" one below)

Encourage shopping malls and
  shopping centers ...._____
Encourage business in existing
  town and city centers ...._____
Don't know / no opinion ...._____

What if the citizenry comes down overwhelmingly against malls? Even if, say, the governor and his administration decide to push hard downtown business, what is to force all the other powers—real estate, commercial, legislative, local, etc.—to abide by a mere poll on the future. Or, if the poll is strongly anti-downtown, how will that affect federal policy, which is clearly in favor of revitalizing the older commercial areas? Of course, if the "don't knows" win or if there is a fairly even split between the malls and downtown, there is no problem—save for the fact that the concept of picking a future has been subverted.

There are other real and potential problems as well. If one is looking for setbacks, problems, and failures in the "Tomorrow/2000/Goals" realm, they are not hard to find. A report on "Citizen Futures Organizations" produced by the Library of Congress's Futures Research Group in late 1976 points to a number of reasons why some of these groups have already failed or faltered. They include poor management, a lack of funds, disinterest on the part of legislatures, inability to involve citizens, and the fact that some were set up to last for a short period of time without any follow-through. Even those groups on the healthy list report problems: low funding, difficulty in getting publicity in the absence of a budget for television programing, unspecified relationships with the established power structure, internal disagreements among different interest groups, and an inability to involve certain elements of the population, such as the very poor, who are naturally more interested in near-term survival than in the state of things in the year 2000.

In terms of longer-range problems the business of involving the public in the shaping of its own future is a serious matter, in that if these studies and plans are merely discussed for a while and then allowed to gather dust, public cynicism is certain to rise. The report on Minnesota's future contains a thinly veiled warning to this effect, in that it spotlights the results of two Harris polls conducted in the state during 1976. In one of them three out of four Minnesotans rated the performance of the legislature as poor or fair, and in the other, 70 percent of the state's residents indicated that they were to some degree distrustful of political institutions.

To some degree this may already have happened, as several ambitious plans have been canceled on the drawing-board or cut off at early stages. An attempt to find out what had happened to the "Ohio 2000" netted this terse reply from a state official: "Unfortunately, and for a number of reasons, this project has been discontinued, and we do not anticipate a revival in the foreseeable future." A very ambitious Colorado Futures Project has been "postponed indefinitely." Ironically, the Colorado exercise was dropped, according to an official involved, because of all of the activities in the state relating to the joint celebration of the Bicentennial and the Colorado Centennial in 1976, a clear case of the past overtaking the future.

Iowa 2000 is another interesting case in point for a different reason. Before the final report was finished, some 50,000 residents took part in the future-planning process through meetings and questionnaires. But when the plan was finished, that was it—no follow-up and no broad-based discussion of how that future was going to be created. The public disappointment was keen enough that the legislature belatedly appropriated some extra dollars to keep the process going, but it seems the steam had already gone out of the citizen-futurist movement in that state.

Yes, But Not Here

This kind of democratic future planning can have ironic results which seldom get alluded to by those who talk about the process in the abstract. In 1973, the progressive administrators of affluent Fairfax County, Virginia, adopted a planning process aimed at controlling the area's runaway growth, which included the massive involvement of citizens through public meetings, questionnaires, neighborhood councils and review boards, and the like. From the outset, the planners committed themselves to following the wishes of the citizenry, which was only fair, since the whole plan had been touched off in the first place because of public outcry against the fact that the pleasant rural portions of the county were being eaten up by housing developments. The commonly expressed fear was that the county would soon be turned into a 400-square-mile tract of single-family houses and shopping malls. There were high hopes for the plan, which was looked at as a "new model" for planning with vast national potential.

However, three years later when the results of this highly ambitious plan were tallied, it was found that one area after another was calling for a solution which would save the countryside by permitting the limited growth of garden apartments and highrises in already developed areas, *but not in their part of the county*. The planners were, of course, totally checkmated, as they had promised to abide by the wishes of the local citizens' groups, and people are still complaining about the continuing consumption of rural acreage by the developers. All of this is reminiscent of a role-playing game used in urban planning courses called "Yes, But Not Here" in which all elements of a community agree on the need for, say, a halfway house for drug addicts and then everyone fights to keep it out of his or her part of town.

In addition to the plans involving the public there are others, framed by those at the highest level of the local power structure, which generally have definite shortcomings. Hazel Henderson uses Goals for Dallas as an example of an elitist plan, which in her opinion has done little more than amplify the voices of the already well-represented and consolidate the power of the politically adept. She adds, "Not surprisingly, it produced the biggest municipal planning disaster of the past decade, the Dallas–Fort Worth Airport."

Upward Movement

Despite all of this, however, the infant movement is exhibiting a true vitality which signals the conclusion that it is much more than a flash-in-the-pan fad of the mid-1970s. Groups that have failed have been re-formed or are in the process of trying to start again. The power structure in Washington is beginning to pay attention (especially Congress); a formal national organization—the Citizen Involvement Network—is in operation to help local futures groups learn from each other. Diverse outside groups, ranging from the League of Women Voters to the National Center for Voluntary Action, have begun to lend their support to the movement. Dennis Little speaks for many observers when he says, "The lesson in all of this is that people are clearly becoming involved in their own futures and in many parts of the nation are already out in front of the traditional planners and politicians."

What is perhaps most remarkable is that the movement has grown and continues to grow spontaneously without any large federal program, massive foundation push, national media attention, or any of the other traditional sparks to new trends. For this reason alone, astute politicians at all levels are beginning to pay real attention. Before becoming President Carter's Secretary of the Interior, Governor Cecil Andrus of Idaho incorporated many of the goals established by the Idaho's Tomorrow program into state plans, and a number of candidates for state office in 1976 adopted program goals into their platforms. Toffler himself says that Senator John Culver of Iowa was elected to that job because of his thoughtful work with the Iowa 2000 project.

While it will take a long time to make a count of true successes in this field because most plans are aimed at the year 2000, it is already clear that some are having a definite impact. The California Tomorrow effort has, by all accounts, gotten many in that state thinking more about the pitfalls of piecemeal planning, and the image of California One has become local shorthand for a chilling and congested future. It is a permanent organization which has followed up on its original master document with reports on specific issues that have had measurable impact, such as its appeal for a strong state program to save the state's coastline, a drive that has been reflected in new legislation. Goals identified by Idaho's Tomorrow have been used by that state in developing land-use legislation, and those running the Dimensions for Charlotte-Mecklenburg in North Carolina claim that 20 percent of the goals laid out for the area have been attained. That 20 percent includes such specifics as the establishment of an independent environmental health program and a full-time director for the local Council on Aging.

Hawaii 2000, which began in 1969, is another effort that did not stop with the publication of its big report on the state's future but is still keeping the debate alive through conferences, course materials, and new publications. A number of outsiders—Margaret Mead and Robert Theobald among them—have commented on the degree to which public consciousness about the future has taken hold in Hawaii.

Alternatives for Washington

The example that Toffler and other proponents of Anticipatory Democracy find most exciting is Alternatives for Washington. It began in 1974 as a one-year effort sparked by then-Governor Daniel J. Evans and the local chapter of the World Future Society. By all accounts, it has grown tremendously in terms of popular support and involvement, and the group is no longer thinking of disbanding. To date it has used a variety of techniques—a statewide task force, questionnaires, area conferences, publications, and a ballot which some 40,000 filled out on the future of the state—to get a consensus. Citizens were asked to react to a number of specific policy questions as well as to pick the future they most wanted from a selection of eleven possible future Washingtons.

The result of all of this has been to create a clear consensus on what the people of the state want and don't want. The state they want is typified by: a responsive, flexible government, a more even distribution of population (read, an end to urban growth), *vigorous* environmental protection, a more diversified and moderately growing economy, new communications technologies such as regional satellites to bring urban cultural advantages to rural areas, and a genuinely "human environment" offering such basics as decent incomes for all citizens. In some of these areas the desired future is quite specific, as, for instance, a new economy built on the state's existing natural resources, which would also include light manufacturing and high-technology industries.

Just as interesting is what they *don't want*, a list that includes the careless use of land, people moving in from other states, racial discrimination, urban sprawl, tax base inequality, the present state constitution (four times longer than the U.S. Constitution), a government that does not listen, and dependence on a few key industries. In terms of the eleven Washingtons offered, the two that ranked last in the poll were "Urban Washington" and "Post-Industrial Washington," which depicted a technological world of service and communications industries. (The ones that polled highest were "Agricultural Washington" and "Balanced Washington," a state combining expanded agriculture and international trade.)

Although the process is still very much in operation—the goals are being refined and priorities set as this is written—a number of important developments have already come out of this exercise in popular futurism. A group of legislators have committed themselves to the plan and are working to convert others. There is now a state-wide movement calling for a new constitutional convention based on the expressed desire of the populace to replace the old constitution. Although it was defeated, before he left office Governor Evans proposed a legislative package which incorporated many elements of the plan, which, if nothing else, advanced the debate on the state's future. Most important, as Nicholas Lewis, director of the program, has stated, "The participants determined what government *ought* to do."

To be sure, Alternatives for Washington has had its share of problems; for instance, some legislators have called it an attempt to circumvent the normal legislative process, and it is now faced with the uncertainty of a new governor, Dixie Lee Ray, who took office in January, 1977. Yet, despite all of this, Alternatives for Washington has become a true force in the power structure of the state.

Alternative Futurists

As examples like Alternatives for Washington demonstrate so clearly, participatory futurists do not forecast the future in the normal sense of the word but are rather prescribing one. One of the major advantages of this approach is at the same time one of its greatest disadvantages: it takes place outside the channels in which future trends are often set. On the one hand, it can lead to fresh and, in some cases, workable futures, while on the other, many trends and developments are beyond the influence of a well-meaning city or state goals group. For instance, a particular future chosen for an area may incorporate policies toward the elderly that are completely within the control of local forces, but may plan an agricultural future that is in direct contradiction to trends established by the Department of Agriculture and the larger national market . . . or that fails to take into account some other factor, such as changing weather patterns.

What this demonstrates is that all three kinds of futurism are clearly interrelated. The participatory futurist says what ought to be, the visionary what can be, and the analytical futurist what is, after all, most likely to be. We will now turn our attention back to the analytic side of the future, starting with some of the techniques used to pick the most likely futures.

4

SPACE AGE FORECASTING
The Old Crystal Ball Has Had It

Late one day, during which I had planned to breeze through a two-inch pile of papers and reports on forecasting techniques, I found myself totally bogged down about halfway through. What had happened was that I kept running into the damndest jargon, technical writing at its most stilted, and plain old infatuation with words of more than three syllables. One of my few triumphs was finding an entry for the *Guinness Book of World Records* under the heading "Hyphenated words, most used in one sentence": "The methodology generalizes the results of categorical-dependent-variable regression, single-equation systems, to correlated, multiple-equation systems of the same form." Later I was to find sentences that put that one in the category of Dick and Jane simplicity.

After that, I began contacting some of the people who were responsible for the reports to ask what they were trying to say and found most willing to translate their findings into remarkably plain English. On more than one occasion, I was told by one author of a complicated paper that he had trouble with the complicated papers others were writing.

All of this is fine up to a point, as experts are entitled to snow each other with their expertise, but many of these same people are the first to complain about nonexperts who do not try to understand the theories of forecasting and are only interested in finding out the date when the first laser hunting rifle will hit the market. Moreover, forecasting is *not* complicated like, say, nuclear physics. It's really rather simple and rooted in common sense.

For the record, it should be noted that a recent survey of the forecasting field conducted by the Stanford Research Institute listed and summarized some 150 techniques. Very few people are acquainted with all 150, let alone the score or more new ones that have certainly been announced since the study was completed in 1975. Actually, only about a dozen are in general use. The fact is that many of the new techniques that get announced and given new names are often slight variations on existing techniques, or as one bemused man in the field put it, "The situation is sort of like those books that promise 150 positions for making love which can only offer so many true variations before they're telling you to move an elbow and claim it as a new position."

Here, then, are some major forms of the art, picked because there's more than a mere elbow's worth of difference between them and explained and expurgated of jargon and technical razzle-dazzle.

1. TREND EXTRAPOLATION

A very common and basic form of forecasting rests on the premise that what happened in the past gives a pattern to what will happen in the future. At the simplest "eyeball" level, some variable is plotted over time as a solid line and the direction of the line projected as a dotted line right into the future following the curve of the established trend. Such simple extrapolation seldom considers limits or external forces on what is being tracked. This can lead to ludicrous results (for example, if you don't consider the limitations of seed, extrapolating the growth of a germinating grass seed will yield a tree). Many wild-eyed forecasts of economic growth or technological progress are based on extending a line with a quick glance at its direction and a flick of the pencil.

However, more sophisticated extrapolation methods have also been developed which take the historical pattern into account and project it as a curve based on a mathematical equation rather than a simple straight line. There are a number of curves and formulas, but all are basically variations on the S-curve which acknowledges limits, leveling-off periods, and periods of rapid growth. For instance, a curve illustrating the growth of the explosive power of weapons would rise steadily through to the end of World War II, jump quickly as nuclear weapons are invented and developed, and then flatten out considerably as the weapons-makers get closer to the limits of killing power—forming an angular, awkward-looking S. The trick here is fitting the best of many curves to the trend being measured. Computers are often used to experiment with such curves.

One does not have to look very hard to find examples of trend extrapolation, as there are few large corporations and no major government agencies that do not deal in curves. When we hear from the Department of Health, Education and Welfare that x amount of doctors will be needed by 1990 or from the Department of Commerce that the average family income in fifteen years will be such-and-such, the figures have come from an S-curve.

The major problem with this technique is that it assumes that the same factors which worked in the past will shape the future. This does not provide for trend reversals and major shifts. The established trend to lower and lower electricity costs and the long-term trend to new cars of increasingly greater horsepower and weight are two recent reversals which have been cited as trends that did not fit the curve.

On the plus side, such forecasts are relatively simple and inexpensive to prepare, quickly understood, and often correct or close enough to being correct to have been worth the effort. As is true of all types of forecasting, an extrapolation that does not come true is not necessarily a bad forecast. If an employer spots a trend to higher and higher employee turnover rates, he may pull out all the stops to reverse the trend.

2. TREND IMPACT ANALYSIS

This is a technique developed by the Futures Group which picks up where trend extrapolation leaves off. After a trend is picked for future study, a computer picks the best-fitting curve from its collection of curves to serve as the base-line "surprise-free" future.

The TIA process begins as a team of researchers come up with a list of events which could have an impact on the trend in question. Events are listed because they are possible, powerful, and unprecedented. They can be suggested by any of a number of sources—other forecasts, panels of experts, the imagination of those on the research team. For every event listed, a probability, time frame, and impact on the trend stated as a positive or negative percentage is estimated. For instance, when the Futures Group looked at the future trend for the number of new drug applications that would be approved by the Food and Drug Administration, the event list generated included these items:

Forecast	Estimated Probability by Year Shown		Maximum Impact on Trend (Percent)
R&D costs in the pharmaceutical industry rise four times as rapidly as the consumer price index for a one-year period	.10	1980	−5
Period of patent protection reduced to five years after market introduction of a product	.20	1990	−3
The time required for regulatory approval of a new drug increases 20 percent over 1970 levels	.40	1985	−3
FDA requires acute, subacute, and chronic animal toxicity tests be completed and evaluated prior to any human testing	.75	1985	−2

Forecast	Estimated Probability by Year Shown	Maximum Impact on Trend (Percent)
Availability of a computer program which uses pattern recognition and cluster analysis to determine the pharmacologic activity of nearly all organic compounds	.80 1986	+8
Availability of automated systems to select the best drug for a specific biochemical disorder (similar to Pfizer's Autobac 1 for determining the susceptibility of various bacterial strains to different antibiotics)	.60 1987	+8
Discovery of a new class of drugs (e.g., drugs to augment immune response, atherosclerotolytic drugs, antiviral agents, etc.)	.70 1984	+18

In addition, time is estimated to the first impact of the event on the number of approved drug applications and the time until the maximum impact. In the case of the last event on the list the time to first impact is five years. On the other hand, the impact of the first event on the list is immediate, so there is no time factor involved.

Once the list and all the estimates are complete, all the information is loaded into a computer, which calculates every one of the probabilities, impacts, and estimates of time. In short, each and every event is permitted to "happen," based on its chance of happening. The result of this major calculation—the heart of the TIA process—is a newly extrapolated forecast line which is often quite different from the original base-line extrapolation. (The new line is a mean forecast, which is usually accompanied by two other lines that give an upper and lower boundary in which the projection is liable to drift.)

One key advantage of this technique is that it strives to

get beyond the surprise-free future and introduce possibilities which are not part of the historical pattern. Another advantage is that the computerized projection that has resulted can be revised, tested, and experimented with. If it suddenly became apparent that one of the items on the list was on its way to coming true well ahead of schedule, the probability might be raised to .95 for the year 1982 from, say, a present rating of .20 by 1990. This would of course affect the direction of the projection. So, too, the system can be used to pose policy questions to see how the projection would be affected if there were a massive industrywide effort to get the automated system in the next-to-last item on the list above into operation in the early 1980s. The disadvantages of TIA are that it is heavily based on the opinions and judgments of those doing the work and that a considerable amount of time is required for the many estimates which must be made for each trend.

The technique is a new one which has generated a lot of excitement but which has had only limited use to date. A major user is the Futures Group itself, which uses it as the basis for its PROSPECTS forecasting service.

3. BAROMETRIC FORECASTS

A catch-all term created here to cover a number of techniques in which some aspect of present reality is used to reveal the future. It is futurism at its most logical and obvious. Included in this category are those who look at the number of new housing permits to foresee the state of the economy or those who look at the number of "Fortune 500" companies working on solar energy research to size up prospects in that field.

A prime example of a group that does this kind of work on a regular basis is the Technology Assessment and Forecast section of the U.S. Patent Office, where each year hundreds of thousands of new patents from all over the world are studied, sorted into tight technical categories, and analyzed for trends. Each year it puts out a thick report on the categories in which current patent activity is the heaviest—presumably and logically an indicator of future development and action. It makes fascinating reading because strong clues to future reality seem to leap off every page. Finding, for example, in the 1976 report, that a number of inventors from different nations have already patented home disposal units that turn garbage into energy for the home is a clear tip-off.

Another example from the same report is a small entry on "plant growth retarders," which has quickly become an area for patent activity by important institutions like Monsanto, Bayer, Eli Lilly, and the Stanford Research Institute. All one has to do to see the potential significance of this entry is to read the Patent Office explanation of what these retarders are intended to do: stimulate seed growth, induce flowering, result in plants with increased resistance to drought and temperature extremes, and create lawns that seldom require mowing.

Currently one of the most exciting centers for futures research in the United States bases its work on the barometric premise. It begs to be described in some detail.

Future Scanning

In the turbulent days of the late 1960s, the president of the Institute of Life Insurance, the industry's social research and public relations arm, decided that the industry should begin looking at the forces that were changing society rather than reacting to them after they had occurred. After some study, it was decided to set up an "early warning system" which would keep tabs on new ideas and changing values. The question, of course, was how do you set up such a system?

The first conclusion made by a special group created to come up with a method was that ideas gave birth to change, and the best system would be one that spotted these ideas when they were fresh. The next conclusion was that the printed words of books, magazines, and newspapers were where these ideas were most likely to crop up, and the frequency with which a new idea showed up in print was seen as a tip-off to what was coming. (TV was written off as a medium that reflects rather than initiates trends.)

Of course, this is basically what an alert, avid reader does (even if it is unconscious), but the group felt it could be developed into a more systematic and reliable technique. The system they came up with, called the Trend Analysis Program, works like this. More than 100 people in various companies which belong to the Institute are assigned publications to monitor (*Harvard Business Review, Rolling Stone, Scientific American*, and so forth). These monitors pick out items which they feel represent a trend, idea, or event with long-range consequences and pass them along to the Institute in the form of abstracts.

Periodically, these abstracts are collected by a special group of analysts with diverse backgrounds who discuss and evaluate them. Some are given special importance if they seem to be breaking a trend (finding, for instance, a cluster of politically conservative articles in traditionally liberal magazines), and sometimes seemingly unrelated abstracts are combined if it is felt they are both part of the same trend. The resulting analyses are then written up in summary form, which typically looks like this example from an April, 1975, meeting:

Artificial Light and Health

Evidence is accumulating to support the contention that if artificial light deviates even slightly from natural sunlight it can have profound and widespread effects on health and behavior. The president of Light and Research, Inc., believes fluorescent light can cause, or at least aggravate, hyperactivity. Preliminary findings suggest that fluorescent light can also be a factor in development of dental caries. One lighting manufacturer is starting to produce light fixtures based on these findings. Some manufacturers of eye-glasses and contact lenses are already modifying products so that they don't block long ultraviolet waves completely.

Others items, nicknamed "straws in the wind," that came out of that same meeting and the one following had to do with such diverse ideas as: the possibility of a syphilis vaccine, a test for the early detection of schizophrenia, experimental farming techniques, and the possibility that there may be a national trend toward legislated ceilings on insurance profits. Sometimes these "straws" are downright unnerving, such as this zinger from a 1976 report:

Ethnic weapons may be developing to eliminate a specific population. An increasing number of differences are being found in blood proteins of various ethnic groups, some of which leave them vulnerable to biochemical weapons. The government denies such research is being done, but neuroscientists are voicing concern.

These bits of analysis are then turned over to still another group, called the steering committee, which in turn uses them to decide on what main themes are involved and warrant being developed into a major report. On the average, all of this leads to about three reports a year, in which a theme is presented in thesis, statistical, and scenario form. Reports issued so far include such titles as "Innovative Technologies in Health and Information Sciences," "Aging and the Aged," "The Employee," and "The Life Cycle."

These reports are characterized by frankness, imagination, and clarity. Punches are not pulled and there is clearly no attempt made to play up to the people who are paying for the reports. Several reports discuss jarring future possibilities for the insurance industry, which have no doubt caused some sleepless nights in Hartford. In a 1990 scenario, for instance, we find that there are no more company insurance agents, but rather free agents working for a centralized service organization run as a joint insurance industry government venture. (A closer look at this scenario can be found on page 222.) A report which dwells on the near-term future up through the next five to ten years talks of such "harsh probabilities" as more trouble for the cities, an irregularity of technological progress (as the secondary effects of new discoveries come under greater scrutiny), international flux, continued challenge to traditional institutions, political turmoil, the extension of the malpractice concept to all professions, and a stop-and-go economy. TAP's unflinching brand of futurism has helped it become one of the most respected of all industry-related futures research groups.

Two natural questions arise from the TAP operation: is its future-scanning technique applicable elsewhere and how useful are its reports? To answer the first, it may well be that there is a certain synergy and imagination at work here, specifically that provided by its director, Edith Weiner, that would be hard to transfer to others, but that is not to say that it cannot be done. The answer to the second question is easier. There is ample evidence that the TAP projections are used broadly in the industry they are created for, resulting in such things as special task forces on the future in individual companies and the use of TAP findings in planning documents and even annual reports. The TAP material has attracted so much attention outside of the insurance field that it is now in the process of altering its own future. By the time of this printing, it should have become an independent research firm serving an expanded list of clients.

4. DELPHI

In the late 1950s two researchers working for the RAND Corporation began working on a technique for forecasting technological developments and events that was based on the premise that a properly selected and questioned group of experts was superior as a source of future speculation to an individual forecaster or even an unstructured group of forecasters trying to come up with a consensus on the future.

The two men who developed the technique, Olaf Helmer and Norman Dalkey, developed it through a series of experiments and gave it the name Delphi—after the famous site at the base of Mount Parnassus in ancient Greece where an oracle did a thriving business making forecasts in response to written questions. Since the original RAND experiments, thousands of Delphi studies have been completed by government groups, corporations, universities, and other institutions around the world.

Typically, twenty to a hundred experts are invited to participate in a Delphi study in which they will be asked to answer a series of specific questions, such as, "By what date do you believe the life expectancy of the average American will reach eighty years?" The experts are asked to answer anonymously, usually by mail, giving both actual predictions and their comments as to why they made the prediction. The first-round forecasts are tallied and the comments are collected and sent back to all the participants who, after reflecting on the feedback from the first round, are asked to answer again. Each person is free to change his or her original estimate or stick with it. The process is repeated several times so that by the final round something close to a consensus judgment is arrived at.

The key to the process is that experts are kept separate and anonymous, which theoretically prevents the estimates from being influenced by such facts as strong personalities, reluctance to change a forecast which has been made publicly, and the "bandwagon effect."

Typically, Delphi results are expressed in terms of dates, percentages, or simple verbal declarations such as "significant increase" or "no change." To get a specific idea of what a Delphi study is likely to yield, here are some specific predictions from a 1964 RAND Corporation study, which was one of the first important examples of Delphi in action. It was conducted by Helmer and Ted Gordon, who now heads the Futures Group, and involved eighty-two respondents, including such important future thinkers as Arthur C. Clarke, Isaac Asimov, inventor Dennis Gabor, and French futurist Bertrand de Jouvenel. The idea behind the study was to determine when certain technological events would take place. In each round the respondents were asked to estimate the date by which they thought a given event or development had a 50 percent chance of being accomplished.

Development	Percentage by which date		
	25%	50%	75%
Implanted plastic or electronic organs	1975	1982	1988
Popular use of personality-control drugs	1980	1983	2000
Controlled thermonuclear power	1980	1986/7	2000
Creation of primitive form of artificial life	1979	1989	2000
Extending life span fifty years by chemical control of aging	1995	2050	2070
Using drugs to raise intelligence level	1984	2012	2050
Chemical control over some hereditary defects	1990	2000	2010

In terms of results, normally the answers that lie at either extreme are knocked out and the forecasts are stated in terms of the median estimate or, in the case of the study just cited, the date by which 50 percent say there is a 50 percent chance the development will have taken place.

There have been hundreds of major Delphi studies conducted since the 1964 RAND study on such subjects as the future of the automobile, energy, chemistry, the aged, social environments, employee benefits, communications, medicine, weapons, and just about any other major topic that one can think of, and a number of minor ones as well. Research groups have conducted a lot of them, as have big corporations (McDonnell Douglas, TRW, Weyerhaeuser, and Smith Kline & French, to name a few), and some have taken on gargantuan national proportions, such as a study of the future of Japanese innovation by the Science and Technology Agency of the Japanese government, which involved no fewer than 4,000 researchers and technical experts. (The Japanese study, which forecast hundreds of individual breakthroughs and technical events, had as one of its major conclusions the opinion that Japan's greatest period of technical innovation would come in the late 1980s.) Americans don't seem to go for such large panels, although 904 experts were recently assembled for a U.S. Forest Service study of "Future Leisure Environments."

While the best-known Delphis are those which look at the future of something, the technique has found a number of other uses. In one of the earliest RAND panels, experts were used to determine how many atomic bombs it would take to wipe out the American arms industry (the final median: 225 bombs), while others have grappled with near-term estimates such as how many people will die in automobile accidents on a given weekend. They have been used to determine the present consensus of the goals or opinions of a particular group—one series of Delphis was used to find what various groups (students, business groups, etc.) felt were the most important factors in personal happiness—and have even been used to look backward to get an expert reading on the importance of historical events. In several cases the technique has been used to get a picture of contemporary social values. A 1971 study conducted by Bell Canada looked at value changes in North American society and found rising, declining, and unchanging values ranging from a significant increase in self-expression to a significant decrease in traditionalism as a value. Materialism remained unchanged.

One of the most unusual uses of Delphi comes in an example provided by the U.S. Army in the testing of a riot-control gun (actually a grenade launcher) which fires a bean bag weighing a third of a pound that temporarily stuns/stops a person rather than doing permanent injury. The Army wanted to know if its stun gun could actually be used without doing permanent damage to the head or the liver without having to test it on human guinea pigs. So it first tested the gun on laboratory animals, photographed the stunned animals, and then presented the pictures to a panel of nationally prominent surgeons who were questioned through Delphi to get a consensus reading on how the animal results translated into human terms —a development which is a more humane alternative to the traditional method of testing nonlethal weapons on human "volunteers."

Delphi is not without its critics, and even those who use it enthusiastically often point to its built-in limitations. Among the most commonly heard complaints are that it suppresses extreme points of view (which may, in the final analysis, be correct) by forcing a consensus, that the question of who really is an "expert" is not clear, that it lacks the stimulation of personal contact, and that the results of studies are often misrepresented. Regarding the last point, studies are sometimes summarized in such a way that one gets the impression that Delphi is a scientific measurement with an extraordinary lock on the future when, in fact, it is nothing more than a system for group conjecture and brainstorming. So, too, many who read and interpret Delphi results tend to breathlessly report that a group of experts has firmly predicted such-and-such by the year 2000, without adding such caveats as that in most cases predictions are based on the date by which the experts feel there is a 50 percent chance of a given development taking place.

One study of the Delphi process, done by Harold Sackman of the RAND Corporation, concludes with no less than sixteen criticisms, ranging from the assertion that questionnaires are often crudely designed to the point that it adds up to "a short-cut social science method that is lacking in minimum standards of professional accountability." Sackman argues that Delphi should either be restudied and upgraded or dropped entirely, and he ends his critique with this thought: "The future is far too important for the human species to be left to fortune-tellers using new versions of old crystal balls. It is time for the oracles to move out and for science to move in."

Such criticism notwithstanding, Delphi has many defenders and is in use by many institutions. In fact, its uses seem to be increasing and moving into new areas. A recent estimate from the Library of Congress's Futures Research Group is that more than 2,000 Delphi studies have been conducted since the early 1960s, which is a significant testament to its acceptance. One clear trend is its growing use among nonexpert groups, which is starting to bring it down to the popular level. Alternatives for Washington, for instance, used a large Delphi to get citizens to refine their thinking on the future of the state, and an ambitious Delphi study is now underway in which garden-variety bureaucrats are being polled to develop a picture of the future of government.

Some experts are working to refine and alter the process, and a number of Delphi variations are being experimented with. Bell Canada, a pioneer in the use of Delphi, has developed an interesting variation called SPRITE (for Sequential Polling and Review of Interacting Teams of Experts), in which the end result is not a consensus of opinion but a diversity of it. The idea here is to get a feel for the range of possibilities and interests that will attach themselves to a potential development.

To sum it up, one is led to think that if one were to conduct a Delphi on Delphi itself among a variety of futurists, the result might be that it has flaws, that it will be improved over time, and that it has already been quite useful in getting an expert's-eye view of the future.

Meanwhile, in the not-too-distant future, there is going to be a need to start following up on some of the earlier studies to see how they are faring with age. There was one check run on the original 1964 RAND Delphi by a researcher at the Institute for the Future who found that of twenty-two events forecast for 1970, fifteen had occurred by that date, five had not, and two were uncertain (in that something had taken place but was not yet commonplace).

5. CROSS-IMPACT ANALYSIS

Delphi and other techniques produce long lists of events and likely dates for them to take place, but do not relate these forecasts to one another. Real world events, of course, do not take place in isolation. Cross-impact analysis (or cross-impact matrices) acknowledges the fact that when certain events take place they tend to speed up or hinder other events.

Although the actual mathematics of this kind of analysis can be fairly complicated, what is actually being accomplished is simplicity itself: if A takes place, what probable effect will that have on B, C, and D taking place? At a simple level, here is an impact matrix which was worked up for the U.S. Army Corps of Engineers. A "0" indicates no appreciable impact, while plus and minus marks indicate an enhanced or reduced probability.

If this event
were to occur

The impact on this event would be

	Lower Population	More Leisure	More Urbanization	More Households
Lower population growth rate		+	−	−
More leisure	+		−	0
More urbanization	0	0		+
More household formation	0	0	+	

Carried to the next level the events are given numerical probabilities, and the process becomes one in which impacts are measured mathematically. Once more than a few events enter the picture, the process is usually handled by computer.

The importance of cross-impact analysis is that it forces one to look at the interrelationships between events. Inconsistencies between forecasts show up and the process often reveals relationships which would not be obvious without it. The technique is useful too as a means of experimenting with ideas to see what effect they have on events—for instance, seeing how the creation of two new three-day weekends would affect the impact of leisure in the matrix above.

6. THE COMPUTER SIMULATION

These tend to have names which sound like the titles of science fiction novels—Globe 6, World 3, Agrimod, Project Cambridge, SEAS (for Strategic Environment Assessment System), and CITY II—typically take years to create, and are seldom low-budget operations. These entities are computer simulations and abound in university research centers and technologically oriented bureaus of government. They have become very hot items in the last few years.

A simulation is basically a computerized replica of some system (the national economy, the coal industry, the toy market, or the human pancreas) into which there has been built a series of mathematical formulas which describe the operation of the system. The set of formulas is the model of the system. The point of a computer simulation is that it can be plugged in and things immediately begin to move faster than in the real world it is simulating. Because of the tremendous abilities of a computer to make the mathematical calculations, a year in the future may be simulated in a matter of seconds.

Computer simulations have two main uses. The first is being given a set of givens on past and present trends and then working out a series of pure and simple predictions. This is basically what was done with the famous MIT World Dynamics model on which the Club of Rome based its prediction that there would be world collapse before the year 2100 unless there are major global limits placed on the growth of population and capital investments.

The second use is experimenting with variables, which is called gaming. For instance, a simulation of air pollution levels might first be instructed to make a prediction for the year 2000 based on a series of present conditions, and then that forecast played with—gamed—as factors like new air pollution control legislation get introduced. Here are two examples of computer simulations intended to show the kinds of things they can accomplish.

Life and Death in a Computer

DYNASIM—for the Dynamic Simulation of Income Model—is a new breed of computer model which was created over a period of seven years at the Urban Institute in Washington. What makes it different is that, unlike most models which deal with things on a large scale, such as the national economy, it deals with the futures of individuals and families, making it a micromodel rather than a macromodel. The premise behind it is that it's one thing to know that the Gross National Product will increase in the coming years if certain policies are followed but quite another to see what those policies will do for the elderly, blacks, women, or the average middle-income family of three. The man who came up with the idea for DYNASIM, Guy H. Orcutt, who is now a professor at Yale, says of it: "Policies should be selected on the basis of their fruit, but it would be preferable to sample the fruit before applying policies to the real world."

Now in operation, the model contains detailed information on 4,000 real Americans picked as a sample from the 1960 census. Based on established rates and trends (life expectancy, birthrate, etc.), it works out future histories for the families and individuals in its sample. This means that inside the computer people have children, move, get divorced, remarry, go onto Social Security, and die. The tricky part of it is they interact and influence each other. If, for instance, a set of parents attains a high level of education, that is taken into account in projecting the educational achievements of their children. All of this is, of course, theoretical, in that the model projects what is most likely to happen to its people over the years. However, the quality of this extremely complex model was tested when it was told to advance the histories of its 4,000 people from 1960 to 1970 and was then checked out against the real information gathered in the 1970 census. In many cases DYNASIM was remarkably close to what actually happened, and in others, where it was not so close, the model was adjusted to get it closer to reality.

Currently DYNASIM is being used primarily to answer

"what if" questions about future factors and policies. Whatever happens to the sample population is then generalized to say what happens to the population at large. For example, DYNASIM has been asked to tell what will happen if the rising divorce rates of the mid-1970s continue into the 1980s. Part of the answer: an increase of a half million new families who will require welfare under the Aid to Families of Dependent Children (AFDC) by 1984. The impact of this would not only be to increase the costs of the AFDC program by an additional $600 million a year, but would have jarring impact on the income differences between households headed by women with dependent children and single males—the former becoming major economic losers of the 1980s and the latter making large income gains.

Other questions it is working on range from what will be the economic impact of women getting wage-rate equality with men to what kind of demands will be put on the Social Security System in the year 2000? The odds are great that DYNASIM and systems like it will become more and more important as the planners and legislators attempt to get a better fix on how their big programs will affect individuals and groups in the future.

The Population Game

This simulation was created several years ago as part of the Duke University Social System Simulation Program. It is a game in the truest sense of the word: a competitive venture among players. Specifically, the Population Game is a role-playing game intended for people administering population control programs on a national level. Its purpose is to give players added experience in making decisions in this complex area where many trade-offs and uncertainties are involved. The general situation at the beginning of the game is, to quote from the player's manual, ". . . roughly equivalent to that which exists in some developing countries. The game is played by three different levels of decision-makers in a hypothetical country. There is one person in charge of the entire national planning effort. His role is to allocate funds which he receives from outside agencies and his own government to the various regions of the country. The regional directors then must allocate their funds among districts which are areas with populations equal to about one million . . . District family planners then decide how they will spend their budgets . . ." Each player is given a description of the area which he administers, for example, District II is a coastal plain with fishing villages whose average family size is six.

As is true in most simulation games of this type, there is no best or correct solution to the game, so you must determine your own goals. If you envision a lower target level for the birthrate in your area, you must decide exactly what level that will be. Of course, players at different levels in the game's bureaucracy will be much more effective if they can decide on compatible goals. Decisions made by the players relate to services which are delivered; money is allocated for such things as the training of nurses in contraceptive methods, the creation of new clinics and hospitals, family planning promotion programs in the mass media, and subsidies to doctors to promote birth control efforts. Each round of the game is equivalent to a year, and at the end of each of these "years" the computer simulates the reaction of the nation and its regions to the decisions. Not only are such factors as births, birthrates, and cost-per-averted-birth computed but so too is population size, literacy rate, per capita income, and death rate—in other words, both the direct and indirect effects of family planning efforts are reported.

The model is sophisticated to the point that it has built-in controls over the simplistic or quick result. For example, at a very simple level, if you put all your money into new hospitals, it will take time to build the hospitals; therefore, nothing will happen for at least a year. Or if you pump all your money into subsidies for doctors, the computer will waste some of the money for the reason that in our hypothetical society some doctors will disregard the subsidies because of personal taboos against birth control.

Besides acting as a training experience the game's developers see it as a way to illustrate by example the need for scientific, systematic family planning. The game has been used in public health administration courses and has been demonstrated to family planners as far away as Korea. (Moving a computer simulation may not be as tough as it sounds—this one is contained in a pile of computer cards eight inches high.)

The advantages of simulations as futuristic devices are many—not the least of which is their speed and their ability to be experimented with—but they also harbor some disadvantages. The most obvious yet most important is that they are only as good as the information which has been used in their construction. In fact, the major criticisms leveled at the World Dynamics model and the gloomy prediction that came with it were that it was incomplete and/or oversimplified. One specific point that has been made by a number of critics is that the simulation left out the factor of feedback—that is, it assumed that as the world learned more and more about its predicament it would do nothing to save itself. Moreover, it has been charged that the model erroneously assumes that resources will be used up at the same rate regardless of their growing scarcity or increasing price.

7. SCENARIO WRITING

Certainly the most readable device for looking at the future is the scenario, which is simply a chronological history written in the future.

The term "scenario" comes from the theater, where it has long been used to describe a rough plot outline, but in the 1950s the word began to be used in a new context as mostly secret "scenarios" began to be written by the RAND Corporation and other military think tanks. The idea was that military issues could be brought into much sharper focus if a series of possible future events were laid out in narrative form—or, as it has been aptly described, military history set in the hereafter rather than the heretofore.

These scripts were not only used to zero in on and think about realistic contingencies of immediate concern (for example, what are the courses of action the Soviet Union might take in the next Arab-Israeli conflict?), but also to force war planners to think about special situations which might not be so obvious (under what circumstances, for example, can you stop a nuclear war once one has started, or at what level of devastation does the United States begin to think about surrendering in a thermonuclear exchange?).

Nuclear War in China

Examples of these military scenarios are not too common because of their classification, but here is one from a collection of Hudson Institute scenarios prepared for the Air Force in the late 1960s which shows what the military brass confronts when given a "what if" proposition in scenario form.

●

The United States invades North Vietnam with an amphibious force of four to five divisions. The intention is to seize the Hanoi-Haiphong area, driving the North Vietnamese government from its capital and destroying its prestige both as a "legitimate" government in the north and as the sponsor of a "winning" insurrection in the south. The invasion succeeds beyond expectations and the authority of the North Vietnamese government begins to disintegrate. The Communist Chinese, led by a militant faction, intervene en masse. As in Korea, the Chinese score important successes in the initial phases, and U.S.-South Vietnamese forces suffer major reverses.

The United States considers alternative policies. Because of the prevailing political climate in the United States and the weight of manpower and material needed, the alternatives of fighting a localized conventional campaign against the Chinese in Vietnam or of a conventional invasion of China itself are rejected. U.S. conventional air power is judged (rightly or wrongly) insufficient wholly to interdict logistics into North Vietnam or to wipe out Chinese industry. Instead the United States detonates a one-megaton weapon at 500,000 feet above Peking as a demonstration together with limited nuclear attacks on selected military targets.

With such attacks the United States is primarily disarming the enemy capacity to harm the United States and targeting the morale of the Chinese people—in an attempt to unhinge Chinese society. It is felt that, subjected to these attacks, the Chinese people may bring irresistible pressure against the regime to compromise with the United States; or alternatively acting out of fear, destroy the regime; or, finally, destroy the regime not so much through purposeful revolution as simply by withdrawing support, Chinese society dissolving into anarchy . . .

The United States then announces the forthcoming destruction (within, say, forty-eight hours) of one of ten (named) cities, simultaneously announcing sanctuary areas. The announcement of ten likely cities is intended to augment the quality of terror and to drive large segments of the population into motion, disrupting or contributing to the disruption of the governmental structure and authority. The announcement of sanctuary areas is intended both as a humanitarian measure and as an important contribution to U.S. peace of mind in the aftermath.

In forty-eight hours the United States delivers a delayed-action warhead or bomb (set for twenty-four hours) in Mukden and simultaneously calls upon the Chinese people to overthrow the regime and save themselves. This attack is followed by similar attacks on three additional cities—Harbin, Changchow, and Canton.

●

At this point the script outline envisions a period of chaos within China which at the least weakens the power of the central government to the point where it must withdraw from Vietnam. The United States then announces, "The Chinese people . . . must under no circumstances aggress or produce nuclear weapons because if they do, the United States will act again."

This scenario, which fortunately did not come true, was just one in a cluster of scenarios in which the researchers look at situations in which nuclear war is started and terminated before all the buttons are pushed. What's more, parallel scenarios were developed to show what reactions might ensue in various parts of the world after the war in question. In one scenario, in which the United States has attacked China with negligible risk to itself, inflicting millions of casualties, a whole raft of possible postwar reactions are looked at, including Japanese revulsion and wholehearted support for what is left of China, European rejection of the U.S., a widespread Third World belief that the war was an expression of American racism, and a host of possible reactions in the United States, including one in which the President who has ordered the war kills himself out of remorse. At one point the scenario is detailed to the point where it describes the plot of an off-Broadway play of great emotional impact in which America's crime against China is reduced to the destruction of a single family. The play, which is about the hopes and fears of this family, says nothing about the war save for the fact that it ends abruptly in the middle of the second act when the bomb falls. The postwar scenario ends with this comment: "A war in which tens or hundreds of millions of Chinese are killed and less than a million or so Americans (are killed) could in fact prove to be a disaster for the United States—even if technically it had won it."

Scenarios of this type are still very popular in military circles (especially at the Studies Analysis and Gaming Agency [SAGA], which creates and runs games for top decision-makers in Washington), but it is just one of a number of kinds of scenario in use today. Presently scenarios are especially popular in futures research, with a major reason for this being that they are particularly versatile. The major disadvantages of the scenario are the degree to which they are dependent on the skill of the author and the ease with which biases creep into the script (although in some cases they are useful in showing a point of view). Here are three major varieties of scenario.

The Synoptic Scenario. Other forms of futures research are often summarized in scenario form to present coherent and readable pictures of the state of things at a certain point in the future. For instance, such scenarios are very commonly used as summaries to Delphi studies, which, without them, would be disjointed lists of dates and developments. Typically they read like this small excerpt from the aforementioned RAND Delphi study which describes the technological world as it might be in the year 2100.

●

Chemical control of the aging process may have been achieved, raising a person's life expectancy to over 100 years. The growth of new limbs and organs through biochemical stimulation may be possible. Man-machine symbiosis, enabling a person to raise his intelligence through direct electromechanical tie-in of his brain with a computing machine, is a distinct possibility. Automation, of course, will have taken further enormous strides, evidenced in all probability by such things as household robots, remote facsimile reproduction of newspapers and magazines in the home, completely automated highway transportation, etc.

The problem of adequately providing the necessities of life for all peoples of the earth will presumably have been solved by international agreements based on the abundance of new sources of energy and raw materials opened up in the 21st century. As for materials, it is even possible that elaborate differential mining processes will have been abandoned in favor of commercially efficient transmutation of elements.

Conceivably, revolutionary developments will have become feasible as a result of control of gravity through some form of modification of the gravitational field.

A permanent lunar colony may well have been established, with regularly scheduled commercial traffic between Earth and Moon. A permanent base on Mars, landings on Jupiter's moons, and manned fly-bys past Pluto are likely accomplishments. Possibly even a multigenerational mission to other solar systems may be on its way, aided conceivably by artificially induced long-duration coma. Two-way communication with extraterrestrial intelligent beings is a definite possibility.

●

The Provocative Scenario. Like military games and scenarios which are used to force military planners to think about certain unlikely situations that could nonetheless occur, the civilian equivalent is a script in which the author begins with a line like, "With the price of gasoline now over $2.50 a gallon, the complexion of the 1980 presidential election has changed considerably."

Such scenarios can be completely fanciful in the sense that they are used to spark thinking in a certain direction or can be based on the logical implications of other forecasts (a number of provocative scenarios could be written based on the forecasts just encountered in the RAND scenario for the year 2100).

The Set of Alternative Futures. Probably the most popular uses of the scenario are in those cases in which a set of them are developed by various means to explore a set of plausible alternative futures. In recent years many sets of these alternative future scenarios have been developed by government and business both for specific items like nuclear power and broader concepts like social norms and the general state of technology. Predictably, great piles of alternative energy scenarios have been created in the last few years by such prestigious institutional authors as the Ford Foundation, the Shell Oil Company, and the Federal Energy Administration.

The importance of a set of alternative future scenarios differs from case to case. Sometimes they are used passively in the sense that they show you the range of circumstances under which you may have to operate. For example, an individual looking at five possible economic scenarios for the U.S. for the next twenty-five years can use them to plan with, but can have no impact on which one comes closest to actually happening. On the other hand, that same set of scenarios in the hands of the President's Council of Economic Advisors can be used to look at the varying impact of different policies and may in fact prompt a decision which changes the course of the future. In some cases sets of scenarios are created to illuminate differences between contrasting policies. Recently the Office of Planning and Evaluation of the Department of Agriculture created three alternative futures based on three different national agricultural policies. It provides an interesting example because it shows how policy decisions made in the near future will affect the nation in the year 2010.

The three futures are:

1. *The Supply Management Future,* in which there
   is strong federal intervention and control to re-
   strict production and stabilize farm income (much
   like the system which existed between 1930 and
   1970).
2. *The Maximum Efficiency Future,* in which all
   government controls and restrictions over the
   production of commodities are removed (somewhat similar to the emerging policies of the early
   1970s).
3. *The Small Farm Future,* in which policies and
   programs are instituted to preserve the largest
   possible number of farms.

In terms of certain key variables, here is how the results of those three policy futures look in 2010, the year
in which the population of the U.S. is projected to reach
300 million.

	#1	#2	#3
Number of farms (millions)	1.50	.95	2.10
Gross farm sales (billions)	$112	$114	$108
Farm labor (millions)	2.8	2.6	2.9
Per capita consumer food costs	$641	$632	$636
Public treasury costs (billions)	$ 1.3	$ .2	$ 3.0

This particular analysis generated much more information than is reproduced here, but just this sampling allows
one to see the advantages and disadvantages inherent in
the three policies.

This agricultural study is just one of hundreds of important future studies which have been conducted in the
last few years. The next two chapters look at some of the
other results of futures research. The first offers a glimpse
of some of the broad-brush alternative scenarios which have
been cast as plausible for America over the next twenty-
five years, and the second examines a large number of
specific forecasts arranged chronologically. Together they
are intended as a showcase for the end product of recent
futures studies and, more to the point, as a useful guide
to the rest of our lives.

5

ALTERNATIVE FUTURES

A State of Tomorrow Report in Which We See That the Future Is a Plural

Visions of the world to come are very much like books, plays, and 45 rpm records—some are hits, some are not. If there were a best-seller list for these visions, the top ten for any given month in recent years would certainly include these:

1. Generally, lousy technocratic and totalitarian anti-Utopias (or dystopias, in the futurist's jargon), with Aldous Huxley's *Brave New World* and George Orwell's *1984* still leading the pack.
2. Variations on the theme of environmental catastrophe. Rachel Carson's *Silent Spring* and all the books, articles, conferences, warnings, and what-have-you that followed.
3. The continuing parade of images which deal with thermonuclear disaster—starting with *Fail Safe*, *On the Beach*, and *Dr. Strangelove*, and leading up to a recent Pentagon estimate that a "limited" nuclear war with the Soviet Union would net 21.7 million dead Americans. (The Pentagon defines limited war as one in which the two nations are merely trying to destroy each other's missiles and do not intend to kill civilians.)
4. A future outside the earth's environment, ranging from *Star Trek*, *2001*, and a good deal of the science fiction ever written to the growing

government and academic interest in space stations and colonies.

5. The belief that unless growth is limited soon, the 21st century will bring with it the collapse of global industrial civilization. This is the view of the Club of Rome, the high-powered international group studying global problems, which is shared by a number of writers, futurists, and resource and population watchers outside the Club.

6. The flip-side to the Club's dire prediction, which says that new mechanisms for limited growth and equilibrium can save spaceship Earth.

7. The fundamentally optimistic view which admits to some shortages and other problems ahead, but promises steady growth in the wealth of nations without bad side effects. The combination of technology and capital will provide and take care of problems as they arise. Herman Kahn, Buckminster Fuller, a number of politicians, and many business leaders are apostles of this future.

8. The gadget and gizmo image, in which social and resource problems are overshadowed by the wonders of new inventions and appliances. This future is exemplified variously by forums on new technology, Sunday supplement writers, glossy brochures and magazine articles on "The Kitchen of the Future" ("The Bathoom of the Future" or whatever), and the popular book *Future Facts*, which describes the world to come in terms of a jazzed-up Spiegel catalog.

9. The Post-Industrial Society (which is also known as the Super-Industrial Society, the Technotronic Era, the Post-Welfare Society, and more, depending on who is writing about it), which describes a state that is already developing but will flower in the next thirty to fifty years. The characteristics of this new society are that it primarily produces services (as opposed to hard goods) and is dominated by a professional/technical class (as opposed to businessmen, who

dominate the industrial society). Daniel Bell and Peter Drucker are the best-known describers of this future.

10. The basically romantic future expressed by the feeling that a proper change in values will lead us to a future in which everything comes out right. It is a utopian hope that is based on people and nations beginning to tolerate, understand, and finally love each other, with the result that war, violence, and other man-made ills die away. This romantic future is portrayed by religious utopians, certain peace groups, highly idealistic liberals, and Charles Reich's *Greening of America*.

There are also a few others which occasionally break into the top ten when events dictate. One of these is the "Factor X" future, in which a random or unpredicted factor either wipes out or completely rearranges the future. "X" can be a worldwide plague, the sudden cooling of the sun, the earth breaking loose from its orbit, or any of a number of other developments. The Factor X theme seems to have a run in popularity after a mysterious happening like the "legionnaires' disease" in 1976.*

The fact that there are so many popular visions of the future kicking around that one can come up with a top ten list not only underscores the difference between the future (what in fact will happen) and futures (what could happen), but suggests the infinite variety of tomorrows that are possible. Just using the ten top futures listed one can come up with all sorts of variants by blending them into, say, a scenario which combines elements of 4, 6, and 8.

Morever, while our top ten futures are useful, they are basically strong caricatures representing some of the more

---

* Other factor "X's" which have gotten recent play: the death of the oceans, the destruction of the ozone layer, the accidental creation of a Frankenstein virus through biological experimentation, nuclear crime, and the emergence of a powerful "insane" nation on the order of Nazi Germany.

dramatic of many possibilities. Currently one of the strongest movements within the futures field is that of creating and studying alternative futures. In fact, if one had the time and patience just to catalog all the different futures coming out of think tanks, government agencies, corporations, and other institutions, the result would be a collection of hundreds of broad societal futures and thousands more which look at the alternative futures of something more specific (energy, food, the Common Market, a city, a state, education, etc.).

What follows is an examination of several major studies which have looked at alternative futures for the United States with one rather stunning example discussed in detail. The examples used are studies created at taxpayer expense for the government but which have received scant public attention.

FLYING FUTURES

Over the years the Federal Aviation Administration has, to put it bluntly, been caught with its pants down on several specific and important issues, one of the most embarrassing of which was that of aircraft noise. By the admission of its own officials, it completely misread the level of public concern on the issue and did not wake up to it until picketers were threatening to close airports, and antinoise forces and public interest groups were hard on the case of the Concorde SST. In other instances, unexpected developments seemed to come out of nowhere, like the rash of airline hijackings and bombings that cropped up in the late 1960s and immediately became the Number One problem of the FAA. Such shocks to the system coupled with the fact that the agency's mandate calls for it to plan the nation's air traffic control system many years into the future promoted it to set up its own internal futures think tank in late 1974.

A team of nine analysts, called the System Concept Branch, was set up to look at the obvious matters of population (how many people will be flying in the year 2000) and technology trends, as well as at the broader social and economic possibilities. Lynn E. Jackson, the man in charge of the group, says, "There is much evidence to suggest that social and economic forces will have far greater impact than technical ones."

One of the first major actions of the group was to commission a major study that would depict a range of plausible futures for America between 1975 and the year 2000 and how the playing out of each script would change the American aviation system. The Futures Group was picked to create the master scenarios, and Urban Systems Research and Engineering was hired on to determine how these scripts would affect aviation specifically.

The actual research involved creating a rather complex hybrid methodology combining several techniques (trend impact analysis, expert forecasting, computer simulation, etc.) to create five scenarios which are plausible, internally consistent, and very precise. In each scenario scores of events and trends are identified as milestones on the course from now until the year 2000. A key element in all of this is a model which simulates the working of the Gross National Product for the year 2000; the model responds by stating how many Americans are liable to board a plane in that year or how much fuel will be consumed by the system. The answers are likely to be strikingly different, depending on the scenario. Under the most prosperous scenario, 850,000,000 barrels of jet fuel get consumed in 2000 while under the least prosperous only 158,000,000 barrels are used (actually lower than the 1974 total of 190,000,000 barrels).

In the briefest possible terms the five socio-economic futures created by the model are:

Limited Growth, in which government acts on behalf of an environmentally conscious public and adopts policies consistent with low population and GNP growth.

Expansive Growth, in which a full return of the free enterprise ethic and unbridled technology create unprecedented prosperity and high growth in population and GNP.

Individual Affluence, which is also a highly prosperous

future but one in which strong government regulation results in high GNP growth and low population growth.

Muddling Through, a future of continued recession, inflation, and uncertainty characterized by low GNP but high population growth.

Resource Allocation, a future in which many of today's pressing problems are solved but prosperity is less than in Expansive Growth or Individual Affluence. This script combines moderate GNP growth with low population growth.

In the final four-volume report on the five futures, each was described in great verbal, statistical, and mathematical detail down to and including such things as air cargo tonnage and the number and type of aircraft accidents in each scenario for the year 2000. Even the number of people killed in commercial aviation accidents is computed. (The fewest die under the worst economic conditions, which is one of the very few advantages of "Muddling Through.") This small sampling of figures from the study gives an idea of how precisely the five possible Americas are described.

Variable	1974	2000: Limited Growth	2000: Mud- dling Through	2000: Re- source Alloca- tion	2000: Indi- vidual Afflu- ence	2000: Expan- sive Growth
GNP (in trillions)	1.3	1.9	2.1	2.9	4.1	4.3
Population (millions)	212	250	297	250	250	297
Unemploy- ment rate	5.6%	6.1%	8.6%	4.8%	4.4%	5.0%
Air passengers (millions)	207	406	272	471	788	1,113

The scenarios and the figures generated with them are *not* intended as forecasts but rather as a range of plausible conditions under which the FAA may have to operate. Their day-to-day usefulness is as yardsticks against which to measure plans, policies, and assumptions.

In the broadest sense they are meant to force policy-makers and planners to see the range of forces which may have an impact on the national air system. If the Individual Affluence scenario is played out, for instance, the power of government will be larger and more persuasive than it is today, whereas if Expansive Growth is the direction in which we are headed, the role of govenment will be greatly reduced. Muddling Through would bring a very low national research and development effort with little change in aircraft technology, while Expansive Growth would bring heavy emphasis on R&D and new technology. In short, it forces people to acknowledge the *uncertainty* of the future rather than any sure bets.

On a more specific level the scenarios are to be used as points of reference for current decision. Quite simply, a plan or policy that only makes sense in terms of one scenario and is mismatched with the other four is clearly more likely to lead to future problems than a plan or policy which fits four out of five scenarios.

All of this is impressive because what the FAA has done with this first major study of the future has been to begin the process of preparing itself for an extreme but realistic set of future scripts. The five futures are definitely not going to be forgotten, but rather used as analytical tools to be judged against the real world. Jackson and his team have begun monitoring outside factors to see which of them are becoming more likely and which less likely. When I asked him if the system was being set up so that it will ultimately be able to find the true socio-economic scenario to the year 2000, he replied, "We're going to try awfully hard."

FEAR OF MUDDLING

Cynically, one can look at this particular exercise and tab it a very expensive piece of pseudoscientific speculation in which great globs of statistical data have been generated for a set of imaginary societies, not one of which will probably come into being as envisioned. This glib response denies the real possibility that studies like this can end up being worth many times their cost if, in fact, they lead to better, more flexible judgments and plans. It also denies a certain small amount of courage which goes along with any group of bureaucrats that mounts a bona fide effort to really think about things twenty-five years from now. Yet if there was some courage behind the effort, there was also some old-fashioned timidity as well.

The basic Futures Group study created something of a flap within the FAA, which as of this writing has not released the whole report for public consumption (although it has released a summary) and will probably only let it out when it has been, as one member of the group terms it, "sanitized."* The fear being expressed is basically that of a cautious public agency which saw some of the details written into the scenarios and recoiled in fear when they realized how they could be misinterpreted out of context.

Now having read the study, the reason for these fears is clear and most vivid in Scenario "D"—Muddling Through, which is actually termed "Hardships" in the original document. The detailed picture which emerges is bleak indeed. Things go downhill from the 1970s, the nation is unable to "get it all together" through the remaining years of this century and enters the 21st "burdened by innumerable problems." To be more specific, the standard of living is down, energy is strictly rationed, life in the cities is "just bearable," unemployment is up, the public is moody and uncertain, world leadership is slipping from the West to the East with China in ascendance, and the government is focusing most of its attention on keeping weak industries alive and has already nationalized a number of them, including the petroleum industry.

In terms of aviation, future conditions in Scenario "D" become so bad that the government has to ultimately take over the air transportation system, including most of the nation's airports. An Amtrak-like monopoly called the National Air Transportation Company is formed which does things like permanently shut down unprofitable airports in smaller communities.

* This was written in April, 1977; the final report was delivered nineteen months earlier in August, 1975.

Even the other more positive scenarios contain their share of developments bound to displease various major interest groups. These include relaxed environmental constraints, increased federal regulation and the decline of the automobile (Limited Growth), the removal of antitrust legislation (Expansive Growth), and suburban sprawl and a high military profile (Individual Affluence).

It takes little imagination to see how the FAA could get into a jam if these details were sensationalized and lifted from context. A headline could be written to read FAA PLAN LOOKS AT POSSIBLE REPEAL OF ALL ANTITRUST LEGISLATION or a member of Congress with an ax to grind could issue a statement that begins, "Thanks to the Federal Aviation Administration, the hard-pressed American taxpayer is now shelling out good money for studies of the year 2000 in which the United States is depressed, demoralized, and ceding its power to the People's Republic of China." (If this seems too far-fetched, it is worth recalling that there is a federal regulation that prohibits any government money from being spent on a study having to do with defeat or surrender—prompted by an historical RAND Corporation study of surrender conducted during the 1950s.)

Nonetheless, the summary of the report, which was released for broad consumption in early 1977, did a good job of describing each scenario without repeating every lurid detail. If there is irony to the cautiousness of the FAA in this matter, it is that some months back the Environmental Protection Agency released but did not publicize the following study, in which there are scenarios that make the grimmest of the FAA futures seem rather pleasant by comparison.

TEN AMERICAS

One of the most fascinating and ambitious examples of scenario building in recent years was completed in the fall of 1975 by the Center for the Study of Social Policy at Stanford Research Institute. The work was sponsored by an obscure unit within the Environmental Protection

Agency (the Strategic Studies Unit of the Office of Pesticides Programs) which wanted a set of possible futures for America to help it prepare for the kinds of varied national environments it could be faced with.

The result of the work is a report with the dry title "Alternative Futures for Environmental Policy Planning: 1975–2000," containing ten detailed scenarios which are anything but dry. Each scenario is written as if it were a letter sent back to the present world by an early 21st-century observer who had just lived through the year 2000. The major "wild cards" have been excluded from the deck (for example, all-out nuclear war, the total collapse of civilization, the growth of a totalitarian dictatorship) for the rather simple reason there would be no Environmental Protection Administration if one of these "wild card" events came to pass. However, lesser wild cards like a prolonged oil embargo and an increased level of political terrorism were included.

In each scenario such variables as climate, food and energy supply, the life style of the individual, the economy, the state of science and industry, ecological values, and social systems are detailed. What they show is an enormous potential for social change which can only be shown with illustrations from each. Following is a brief summary of each along with significant excerpts from each "social systems" section, which is consistently the most revealing section. Before going on, however, three terms that are used in the scenarios to describe specific value systems should be defined in advance. *Achievement values* refers to those that emphasize material things on the personal level and growth, bigness and competition on the larger level. *Survival values* are those held by people who embrace "achievement" values but cannot realize them because of material circumstances. *Frugal values* are, to quote the study, those based on the "voluntary simplification of the exterior aspects of life in order to attain greater richness of inner aspects."*

* Although the report is in the public domain and therefore usable without permission, both the Stanford Center and the official at the Environmental Protection Agency who was in charge of the project

SCENARIO 1

"Hitting the Jackpot"

All goes well. There is abundant energy, widespread prosperity, highly responsible business leadership, world-wide environmental cooperation, and a scientific community able to contend with most of the earth's technical problems. Even nature acts kindly, providing favorable climate and plenty of food.

Social Systems

The United States and the other free-market industrial countries demonstrated the will, vigor, and capacity to meet the challenges posed by the near doubling of world population, pressure on natural resources, shifts in the global political balance, and the problems of economic development in the Third World. This material success had the effect of reinforcing existing social values in the West and bringing about their further acceptance elsewhere.

The process of urbanization continued. Rural populations declined even further from their already low levels in the West and, through a combination of drastically lowered birthrates and rural emigration, were reduced throughout the world. Vast investments in housing, sewage systems, and other public utilities, and the expansion of health, fire and police, and social welfare systems went far to solve the physical problems of the urban environment. Characteristic of the urbanization process was the development of numerous satellite cities which repeated, on a lesser scale, the apartment style of living that almost universally replaced the single home suburb, even in the United States.

The nuclear, single-generation family remained the

were contacted and expressed enthusiasm for having it quoted selectively here. The full report (complete with the full scenarios, which fill more than 200 pages) is available on request through the Environmental Protection Agency, Office of Pesticides Programs, Washington, D.C. 20460. The document number is EPA-540/9-75-027.

norm in the West and in the modernizing sectors of the rest of the world. The much lower birthrate— partly a function of a much later formal marriage age —made child care and education a less pressing concern for society than the provision of health and welfare services for the burgeoning older-age groups. With high economic activity and less physically demanding jobs, it proved possible and desirable to raise the retirement age to 70. However, despite advances in geriatric medicine that allowed the very affluent in the more advanced countries to extend their lives greatly, more and more of the nonaffluent elderly chose to reject life-prolonging technology and even to accept forms of geriatric euthanasia as a socially acceptable means of terminating existence . . .

As great corporations became ever more dominant in the economy, their societal role expanded. The Japanese model of lifetime employment [for the same company] increasingly came to be the norm . . .

SCENARIO 2

"Not-So-Great Expectations"

A decline in energy supply, worsening climate, and food shortages combine to create a major depression in the mid-1980s. Accommodations are made and our social and economic institutions survive. There is economic recovery in the 1990s, albeit less affluent than previous recoveries, and the first years of the next century are characterized by an adaptation to temperate, resource-conserving behavior. A major factor in making all of this work has been the growth of a sizable minority of "frugal people" who embrace such things as an intense personal concern for conservation, backyard gardening, and other "technologies of scarcity" as their life style—basically, an extension of the values first expressed in *The Whole Earth Catalog*. With the arrival of the year 2000, American society is deeply split between two value groups: the frugals and the traditional achievement-oriented consumers.

Social Systems

The early 1980s was a time of very rapid change as the enormity of the failure of the economic policy of the late 1970s struck home. In all the countries experiencing the changes for the worse associated with this scenario, there was much irrational social behavior. During the 1980s particularly, crime, family breakdown, alcoholism, narcotics abuse, bizarre religiosity, and suicide became more and more common. Stability and rationality were associated with those who adopted the frugal values and, in the 1990s, with the reemerging achievers. The directors of the failing society of the 1980s, although themselves demoralized, were rational in their determination not to resort to war. The 1980–1990 decade was one in which everything malfunctioned—even the weather. Power outages, transportation breakdowns, crop failures, and shortages of raw materials, and spare parts were characteristics of the economy. Those choosing the survival ethic responded by ripping off and ripping down—squatting in abandoned buildings, begging, pilfering, and ultimately accepting the barest conditions of survival as enough. The frugals responded by organizing modest productive activities, community services, repair and maintenance programs, in order to supplement or replace what the traditional government or economic institutions could no longer deliver with regularity. After 1990 there was gradual improvement. Demands on the system were no longer so great, nor expectations so high. The sense of independence and the means for independence from the system were greater and more developed. Hence the complex and nearly automatic production and delivery means characteristic of the pre-1980 period fell into disuse. The simpler, less automated system did not function with as great speed or efficiency—but it broke down less frequently and was more easily restored when it did.

The technocratic ethic of complexity and highly

specialized knowledge diminished throughout the whole period . . .

There was throughout a consensus on the need to avoid worsening the situation by war or revolution . . .

. . . There was little production of surplus. Even the frugals did not consider themselves obliged to take care of those who would not take care of themselves. Both the new achievers and the continuing body of directors who had kept the system (mal) functioning during the darkest days of the 1980s aided the survivors only out of the need for self-protection, and as a supplement to the use of police force.

SCENARIO 3

"Apocalyptic Transformation"

In this scenario American society comes very close to collapsing but makes it through by creating a new social order in which the frugals become the major force in the society. What has happened is that the United States commits itself to high growth and ever-rising affluence and continues to expend its resources to achieve these goals. It works for a time, but in the mid-1980s two major events shatter the dream. The first is the "energy bust," in which we start running out of energy at a point when technology is still unable to come up with new sources, and the second is a markedly deteriorating climate. By 1990 the average American is just getting by. With the large-scale adoption of frugal values and practices and a few good years in the 1990s, the general outlook in the year 2000 is hopeful.

Social Systems

America marked its Bicentennial Celebration with a determination to take the traumatic events of the first half of the 1970s in stride. It declared it would resume its leadership of the free world nations.* Prophecies of gloom were not to be heeded. The

* This did not happen as such but has happened to some degree in 1977 with President Carter's human rights initiatives.

economy was to be kept going and the high consumption life-style maintained. In the meantime, the effort to discover new energy sources, funded substantially through federal deficit financing, would, it was believed, make Project Independence a reality within ten years . . .

Within five years the dream was shattered. The nuclear energy program had to be abandoned after a series of disasters related to nuclear waste disposal and one spectacular catastrophe resulting in tens of thousands of deaths in an accidental Hiroshima. Likewise, a discouraging string of offshore oil spills on the U.S. East Coast combined with an OPEC policy of restricting exports of oil in the interest of maintaining reserves for burgeoning industry in the Middle East and Latin America brought about an energy bust that coincided with the beginning of several years of disastrous weather.

Industry in the United States and older developed countries nearly collapsed. Food shortages and utility breakdowns brought about near social collapse as well. The frustrations erupted into armed quarrels among old enemies and erstwhile friends in a dog-eat-dog competition for access to oil, food, and raw materials.

Fortunately, despite the use of tactical nuclear weapons in these struggles, the ultimate holocaust was not unleashed. However, the international order was shattered. Within the United States and elsewhere central authority became weak and ineffectual, and the period of near anarchy extended into the 90s . . .

The major social system characteristics of this future for the most part can be described as a desperate clinging to traditional forms even in the face of their inadequacy . . .

During the 1980s, democracy, both as a social expression and a political ideal, declined. Even as government became less effective it became more authoritarian and arbitrary . . .

The condition of the survivor sector was so bad

that by the early 1990s more than a third of the U.S. population characterized by survival values had just about lost social coherence. The worst features of the so-called culture of poverty—family breakdown, mass criminality, drug addiction, alcoholism—were epidemic in this sector. One of the most demanding tasks of the new society emerging by the end of this scenario was the rehabilitation and reintegration of this demoralized group into productive life.

By the end of the century the situation was one in which the frugal ethic and life-style had come to dominate. The inflated expectations that had marked the beginning of the era had been abandoned. The frustration, with its violence and irrationality, that had marked the 1980s had given way to a determination to make the best of things. While the ideal of one world, of spaceship Earth, now seemed unattainable, the widely shared frugal ethic did allow for the lifeboats to take people on board and to move in a sort of convoy . . .

SCENARIO 4

"Journey to Transcendence"

Ever-growing rates of inflation and unemployment lead to inevitable annual drops in the national standard of living. Determined attempts by the nation's leaders to make the "American dream" come alive in the face of these other conditions appear increasingly futile, and gradually the new frugal ideal takes hold. By the year 2000 Americans have learned to live comfortably within new limits.

Social Systems

The world in 2000 looked so different from that which had existed in the mid-1970s that an older generation had difficulty in explaining to a younger what had been and in explaining to itself how the change had come about . . .

Within the United States, western Europe, and Japan the sense of crisis (of the early 1980s) produced governments of national unity able to impose systems of controls on energy use and other forms of consumption and to organize massive programs for the development of new energy technologies. Awareness of the size of the problem induced them [i.e., the world's governments] increasingly to pool their resources and internationalize their programs. Paradoxically, the growth of national and supranational unity was accompanied by the flourishing of diverse life-styles. [Frugal] Individuals and communal groups, even while cooperating with the national effort, were increasingly active in devising new responses, both economic and social, to the imposed austerity. Such responses typically were marked by more individual and group self-reliance, ingenuity, and tolerance. As the 1980s wore on without achievement of the technological successes that had been hoped for . . . these frugal groups and individuals, while still patiently supporting the continuing efforts of the governments, grew markedly in numbers and influence . . .

In effect, a parallel system (or systems) of self-governing, self-regulating communities concerned with both economic survival and personal growth expanded alongside the faltering but still functioning structure of corporate manufacturing and service. For the older generation, particularly, the experience was one of reduced expectations and defeat, but for many, even in that generation, the experience was positive and liberating. Although these communities showed a diversity of forms and styles, the overall trends was toward homogeneity as informal communications networks transmitted the news of what worked and what did not. It was the existence of this network that ensured against the shattering of national economies into isolated, feudal pickets. Major elements of the surface transportation system, for instance, became owned and maintained by frugal cooperatives in the 1980s and 1990s . . .

Gradually and unofficially the lineaments of a post-industrial, low-growth, diversified, and decentralized world system were taking shape even as official faith was maintained in a return to the old system once the energy breakthrough occurred. However, by the late 1990s, elections in the United States, Europe, and Japan revealed that the old system was just about defunct . . . The post-industrial system, committed to low technology, small is beautiful, humane and self-fulfilling goals and a spaceship Earth philosophy, had emerged . . .

SCENARIO 5

"The Center Holds"

Despite energy shortages, bad climate, an eroding living standard, and a wholesale increase in acts of political terrorism in the 1980s, the established order of big business, big agriculture, and big government is able to retain its power and control (although at times the establishment seems unable to cope with its problems). Some good weather years and technological breakthroughs on the energy front enable these big powers to hold onto the world system of the 1970s in the year 2000, but the system is now more authoritarian and highly regulated.

Social Systems

The basic societal institutions of the free-market industrial nations—particularly the United States—came under severe stress, appearing at one point to be on the point of disappearing, but were clung to by a majority of the people throughout and, in the end, retained in modified form when the many alternatives proposed to them were shown to be even less adequate to [deal with] the crises of the period. The nation-state as the major focus of loyalties, the nuclear family, extended education, the job-income nexus remained the context in which most people expected to live their lives and through which they would gain their rewards. Big cities, big industry, and big government, all relying on big and complex science and technology, remained throughout the period. Although saving, deferred gratification, and self-reliance remained the major [professed] social virtues, in actuality a . . . welfare state made personal savings less important, while a permissive, high-consumption materialist ethic both discouraged saving and encouraged instant gratification. Perhaps the societal change that made the most visible difference was the decline in private automobile ownership. Another was the decrease in private home ownership as more and more Americans adopted the European style of apartment dwelling in large cities rather than owning the detached suburban house. These changes added to the sense of increasing homogeneity among developed world societies.

The variety of competing economic and societal systems (that were actually fairly similar) operated through the medium of the nation-state. Throughout the 1980s the dominance of the nation-state ideal over that of international order contributed to a low-level conflict situation being generalized. Cold war occasionally kindled and flared, but the threatened general conflagration never resulted. By 1990 the turbulence subsided into a form of general, but wary, world détente . . .

Before that, however, the competitive world situation, combined with frustrations resulting from the depressed economic conditions of the late 1970s and early 1980s, was expressed in irrational political and social behavior. More than one act of nuclear terrorism occurred. The more familiar varieties of socio-political violence became endemic—assassinations, political kidnappings, massive sabotage, capital frauds, autonomous police repressions, military coups, crop and livestock destruction, strikes and lockouts. The association of such acts with all groups, both violent and nonviolent, who were advocating social change resulted by the 1990s in massive rejection of change and a determination to restore order along the old familiar social lines.

The beneficiaries of this determination were the

traditional elites of government and big business with their allies in academia and the military. The informal terms under which this leadership agreed to assume responsibility during the "reaction" of the 1990s included political reform that limited popular participation in the decision-making process and reduced the power of mass political parties; resumption of scientific and technological activity subject only to their control; and an end to egalitarian policies designed to reduce income and wealth differentials.

By 2000 the "establishment" was more firmly seated than ever and the political process was more restricted in most countries than before . . .

SCENARIO 6

"The Boom Years"

Because of an inability to deal with growing energy problems, the United States is in the midst of a long and deep recession by 1980. But an improving climate and the arrival of new energy sources (coal gasification, safe nuclear power, and limited solar and geothermal advances) bring dramatic improvement by the year 1990. The frugal people who had grown in number during the recession dwindled back to a small minority, and by the turn of the century there seemed to be no limits to growth and individual affluence.

Social Systems

Breakthroughs in energy technology came about by the mid-1980s. Achieved almost simultaneously by national energy projects in the United States, Japan, the Soviet Union, and in western Europe, the new technologies freed the industrial nations from dependency on Third World sources of fuel and, even more significantly, allowed the working of such lowgrade ores as to establish self-sufficiency in raw materials. The result was the initiation of a new binge of industrialization and economic growth, free not only from any necessity for national competition but from any real necessity for international interdependence, trade, or cooperation. On the other hand, even as each industrial nation eliminated poverty and reached levels of general affluence . . . the surplus available to distribute in programs for the poor nations amounted, almost, to the realization of people's wildest dreams. By the year 2000, the Age of Affluence dawned. Scarcity was a word without current significance . . .

The world political map remained unchanged. Even the smallest nations were economically viable: each could indulge in the luxury of an individual, national life-style. However, since the optimizing principle of one best way predominated, the highly materialistic mode of life tended to reproduce itself almost everywhere . . .

Within the nations the major problems of societal adjustment lay in coming face-to-face with the utopian issues of affluence and leisure. Through the 1990s the swing back to the achievement values implied renewed commitment to the traditional principles of work, striving for advancement, making the most of the new opportunities. By 2000, however, a major shift toward more hedonistic, experimental life-styles was underway. On the one hand, enormous creative energies were released and more and more people sought both personal liberation and cultural achievement. On the other hand, a pathological, asocial, self-destructive side of human nature expressed itself more and more in meaningless crime, alcoholism and drug addiction, cultism, superstition, boredom, and high rates of mental illness and suicide. While the high prosperity of the era made these outcomes relatively tolerable and victimless crime was no longer prosecuted (consenting adults could live highly individual and even bizarre lives), controlling elites were worried enough to begin to devote research to genetic engineering, psychological, and psychochemical means for keeping the population within bounds of acceptable behavior.

The dominance of great corporations and the relative weakness of government, plus the development of [employee] stock distribution plans, tended to produce a form of corporate citizenship. This was not industrial democracy; on the contrary, corporations continued to be elite dictatorships . . .

SCENARIO 7

"The Industrial Renaissance"

The ineptness of the country's leaders in controlling energy consumption touches off an early 1980s recession and a subsequent curbing of economic growth. A rich, new energy technology comes on line in the nick of time and rapid growth becomes the order of the day for the late 1980s. The scientists, engineers, and planners who had rescued society gain much greater power and credibility and are able to impose on the majority their view of a finite earth not able to stand rapid growth and waste. In 2000 this technological elite has created a nonwasteful, nonpolluting America with a purposeful goal of slow growth.

Social Systems

The social systems of the United States and the rest of the industrial (and industrializing) nations passed through twenty-five years of rapid, but largely easy and smooth, continuous change. The disarray of the mid-1970s, marked by oil, food, monetary, diplomatic, and military crises provided an unpromising beginning for this change . . .

By 1980, though, and especially in the United States, public patience with watching and waiting for the new dawn had begun to wear thin. Rationing and control systems were being evaded, and the promised breakthroughs in new energy technologies—viewed as the key to all problems—seemed as far away as ever . . . Then there came major breakthroughs in nonnuclear energy technology—coal gasification and oil shale processing, particularly, coupled with the exploitation of new offshore oilfields. These triggered a resumption of intensive industrial activity and a general achievement-orientation in society at large. Very quickly the whole system of controls and restraints was jettisoned.

The demonstration of renewed strength in the traditional industrial societies did a great deal to restore their international prestige. The multinational corporations, which had declined relatively during the previous ten years, found themselves being courted by the struggling new industries of the OPEC countries. Other developing countries began to renew and revive their connections with Europe and North America. A spirit of cooperative internationalism marked the era . . .

Even during this period of renewed expansion the elites within the industrial countries did not return to the old, unbridled quantitative growth ethic. For one thing, they were aware that the new resources were no more infinite than the old had been. For another, they accepted the warnings of scientists about the environmental hazards of the industrial process generally. Elite business and government leaders (usually indistinguishable) saw themselves as the responsible stewards of the earth . . .

The norms of social organization characteristic of the industrial countries of Europe and North America tended to predominate worldwide. The nuclear, one-generation family, usually with two or fewer children, became the average. Populations stabilized or even began to decline. Urbanization continued, but better-planned satellite cities of manageable size tended to replace the sprawling conurbations of previous years. The apartment house more and more replaced the detached single family house as the usual dwelling, but parks, municipal gardens, community workshops, and so forth were adequate substitutes for home workshops and gardens.

SCENARIO 8

"The Dark at the Top of the Stairs"

Generally, things go from bad to worse. Seemingly unending bad climate and recession lead to a withering of the Western industrial states in the later years of the century and the grudging acceptance of a starkly frugal life style. The dominant worldwide mood in the year 2000 is one of pessimism. The industrialized world is near total exhaustion, the socialist world no better off (although less traumatized by deprivation), and most of the Third World has relapsed into a primitive state.

Social Systems

Despite a determined effort through more than two decades, this scenario concluded around 2000 with a situation in which the bleak visions of Robert Heilbroner, Paul Ehrlich, and Harry Browne were at least partially fulfilled. The stubbornness with which the industrial nations, especially the Western ones, maintained their faith in the viability of their major institutions was amazing, if only because there were so few and small successes to offset the steady sequence of failures and dashed hopes.

This was an intensely rational period at first. It became clear in the mid-1970s that the political and economic balance of the post–World War II world had changed and was changing irrevocably to the disadvantage of the so-called free world of the industrial nations and their Third World dependencies. Thus national planning agencies in the United States, Europe, and Japan—at first independently but increasingly on a coordinated and cooperative basis—developed programs of austerity designed to hold their systems together pending the technological breakthroughs that would provide new sources of energy and restore growth to their economies. Vast amounts of capital supported by very high taxes went into these programs . . .

The increased adaptiveness and ingenuity developed

by many individuals led to a growth in the numbers adopting a frugal ethic even while most did so in the name of supporting the achievement ethic. Since full employment—at lowered wages and in government makework programs—was maintained, an equal number of people were unwittingly conditioned in the survivor ethic. Thus, despite the appearance of high consensus and homogeneity throughout those dogged decades, society was actually becoming more heterogeneous, and the commitment to the controls applied from the top was weakening. Also, a formally rigid society was actually becoming increasingly adaptive. On the one hand, frugals developed satisfactory alternative life-styles that allowed them to escape the effects of the rules. On the other, survivors hustled, black-marketed, and managed to beat the system. Thus within a highly collectivized system a wide range of individual styles became visible. As the 90s wore on, fewer and fewer people had any real commitment to the achiever program. Officially programed activities became sterile and failed to succeed enough to sustain the faith . . .

What tipped the balance was the impact of the bad weather cycle of the 90s. Cold weather and food shortages caused abandonment of controls on fuels. Central authority everywhere tended to break down. International agreements were abandoned, and not amicably, as the various nations accused each other of violations. The erstwhile passengers on spaceship Earth took to their individual lifeboats and drifted away from each other in an increasingly cold and dark climate . . .

The more favored regions, where alternative economies based on "small is beautiful" had been built up imperceptibly by frugals, began to adopt policies of "caring for our own . . ."

Just as the shift to a controlled and centralized economy in the 70s and early 80s had been rapid, so was the turn to decentralization. Even more sudden was the abandonment of faith in science and technology and the corollary commitment to universal humane idealism. Big science, big technology had failed; the vision of a renewed march toward affluence for all became a mockery. Frugals, in a variety of societal forms, lived in islands of relative prosperity in favored regions. Survivors, almost equal in number, formed a vast urban and rural proletariat living in an Appalachia-like poverty culture marked by debased versions of traditional forms.

SCENARIO 9

"Mature Calm"

Clear failure to come to grips with increased demands for energy brings on a bad recession, requires many to live frugally, which in itself lessens energy demands and begins solving the problem. With the aid of favorable climate, the country's leaders have things under much better control in the 1990s and living standards are again rising. Inevitably, many of those who had become frugal out of a sense of self-preservation were coming back into the traditional consumer mainstream.

Social Systems

There was a relatively smooth transition to a . . . postindustrial future by the year 2000. However, this future by no means displayed the super affluence envisioned by Herman Kahn . . .

The world order was far more homogeneous than pluralist and grew more so throughout the period. Birthrates stabilized worldwide at bare replacement levels and while there were, to be sure, rich and poor nations, in all of them a modernized middle class became prominent and set the tone and style of society. These middle classes were linked through the multinational corporate network that, through the joint venture organization, extended even into the East European communist countries . . .

Increasingly the utility of the nation—state and its emotional holding power diminished. By 1990, most nations dealt internationally through regional confederations. The seas and their resources were completely internationalized under United Nations control and national surface navies disbanded. The experience of regionalization contributed to further dissipation of the nationalist ethic so that by 2000 the prospect of actual world government—at least for the purpose of providing policy guidance to the national and regional confederations and for administering the rules of international trade—was viewed as imminent, inevitable, and desirable.

Although the period 1975–1980 was one of disappointed hopes for technological breakthrough in the energy area and was marked by a sluggish and recessive economy in the United States and elsewhere, there was never any suggestion of collapse or real fear that it might occur . . . The atmosphere in the United States was one of sober rationality. Failures were taken in stride; goals were limited and realistic. From 1980 onward the number of people who adopted frugal values increased. A renewed period of good climatic conditions worldwide allowed the utilization of formerly marginal agricultural land, and there was a visible back-to-the-farm movement by both individuals and cooperative or communal groups . . .

While the growing ranks of the frugals produced a variety of life-styles—diverse forms of family organization, distinctive dress and diet, rituals, architectural forms, literature and entertainments—that allowed them to be distinguished at a glance from the achievers who clung more or less tenaciously to the norms of the "straight" society of the 1970s, both groups shared more concepts than they held differing ones. Even by 1990, when American society was almost evenly split between the two groups, they were both committed to individual human dignity, awareness of the finitude of resources and the need for preservation of the biosphere, faith in the rational process, insistence on peace between nations and domestic law and order. Their essential difference was the frugal acceptance of a stable economy in which concentration was on qualitative growth versus the achiever faith that a "normal" technology-based, industrial-growth economy had to be restored . . .

Change was relatively slow during this quarter century, but continuous. Looking back from 2000, people were astonished at how much change there had been. There was a sense of accomplishment but not smugness . . .

SCENARIO 10

"Toward the Jeffersonian Ideal"

The key factor in this future is the rapid shift in the values of the average American, who quickly realizes that he or she must temper the urge to be affluent with the realities of limited resources. On January 1, 2000, the average American is a frugal person who fully understands the need for such national policies as the one that dictates zero energy growth for the foreseeable future.

Social Systems

Through the period 1980 to 2000 there was very rapid yet smooth and continuous change in social systems in the United States and the rest of the industrialized world toward a state which resembles the "greening" popularized by Charles Reich in *The Greening of America* and discussed by Dennis Gabor in *The Mature Society*.

People showed an enormous resilience as they realized by the early 1980s that there would not be a return to the wide-open economic growth that characterized the heyday of industrialization . . .

Consistent with this process of adjustment, the nation–state remained the primary political and emotional unit in international affairs. However, there was at the same time a strong commitment to international peace and order which . . . was expressed in the subordination of perceived national interests to world interests . . . (and) much of the social rigidity connected with concepts of mastery over nature and of private property rights tended to dissipate . . .

Another important social characteristic was the high degree of activism . . . (as) more and more people learned to cope and regained a sense of control over their lives. A visible minority strove to become economically self-sufficient either alone or in communes; more people demanded a voice in the management of more traditional economic enterprises. Both groups formed a confident citizenry, skeptical of "experts," and became in every way more resilient and self-reliant. This was definitely a mature society in which the principle of "consenting adults" applied in almost every sphere of living.

As the achievement sector diminished in importance, the trend to urbanization was reversed. The relatively self-sufficient small town and city gained renewed importance. Many of the farm communities that had declined during the mid-20th century revived, but increasingly displayed features of the European agricultural village rather than the American farm town. Most of the frugals who went back to the land during this period adapted industrial division-of-labor techniques both to farming and the integrated low-technology industries and services of the farm towns. Frequently, they designated their enterprises as companies or corporations and employed participative techniques of democratic industrial management. Others, more frankly modeling themselves on Hutterite or other communal agricultural communities, called their towns and their enterprises communes, collectives, or cooperatives. While there was considerable experimentation with a variety of basic social forms, the extended biological family tended to predominate . . .

By the old economic rules, this was not . . . a period which one could call successful. However, survival with self-respect intact became itself the measure of success—and came to be preferred to affluence at the expense of self-respect . . .

Collectively these ten visions of the American future are dramatic and provocative. In nine out of ten of them (all save the first), trends that have been taken for granted for a long time are turned around, producing deep social change, and in terms of the thinking of the majority of Americans now living, there is very little good economic news spread through them. If there is anything reassuring it is that the research team concluded that there was only a low probability of thermonuclear war or major armed conflict between the developed nations. (However, the researchers did assign high probability to international conflict and civil war between and within the underdeveloped nations.)

Two questions seem appropriate here. How did the research group come up with these particular images of the future and how useful are they?

The study approach did not conform to a standard methodology but was rather prepared by going through these four steps: (1) From a large list of trends which could have an impact on the future, eleven were selected for detailed study. (2) Four trends—energy, climate, food, and social values—were picked as "driving" trends with particular influence on the future. Rough "skeletal scenarios" were written around these trends. (3) A survey was made of futures literature to gather a broad range of future views and images. (4) The final ten scenarios were developed as the "skeletal" versions were fleshed out with views and visions from the futures literature.

What distinguishes it from other works is the conscious attempt made to incorporate a broad range of future views —from research reports to science fiction and from the hopeful Herman Kahn to the dire Robert Heilbroner, who basically thinks that there is no hope for mankind (or at least that is what he says in his 1974 book, *An Inquiry into the Human Prospect*). The net result is, therefore, a set of scenarios which serve as a state of the art blending the major—albeit diverse and, often, diametrically opposed— views of the future into a coherent package. Unlike an Ayn Rand novel, the point is not in trying to figure out what thinker or school of thinkers fits into which scenario, but to realize that it is a remarkable summary which in itself goes a long way toward answering the question of the usefulness of the study.

It is, however, interesting to note parenthetically that Willis Harman, founder and associate director of the SRI Center for the Study of Social Policy, is clearly associated with a specific future outlook which is based on his research at the Center; yet his outlook does not dominate the study. Harman's view of the future coincides to varying degrees with three of these scenarios. He sees our industrialized civilization in deep trouble—a condition he terms the "world macroproblem"—and that in response, Western society is beginning to go through a profound transformation. Two new complimentary "ethics" are characteristic of this coming break. One is a true ecological transformation in which the limits to the earth are fully realized, and the other is a "self-realization" ethic that asserts that the individual's largely untapped human potential is all-important. To varying degrees this transformation is visible in "Apocalyptic Transformation," "Journey to Transcendence," "Toward the Jeffersonian Ideal," while in the other six the values of the industrial age prevail and succeed or fail but there is no transformation.

The question of the usefulness of the scenarios can also be answered on other levels. They have been analyzed by the study group to see the policy implications common to most (but not all) and what those implications mean to the future of the Environmental Protection Agency. Based on their "cross-scenario analysis" it was concluded that the EPA would have a rough time realizing its goals over the short run (through 1985), a smoother time in the intermediate future (1985–1995), and excellent prospects in the long run. Such analysis is used in turn to discuss the agency's strategy options for the future. If, as is suggested by some of the scenarios, there is going to be some antienvironmentalist feeling in force through to the late 1980s, says the report, ". . . it would seem that a strong regulatory posture and policy may not only be ineffectual—given the lack of public support—but it may also result in the reduction of EPA capability to act effectively in succeeding periods." A possible option suggested by this would be for the agency to concentrate on maintaining its credibility, strengthening its resources, and getting ready for a period of activism in the late 1980s.

While it is very hard to determine how such analysis will actually affect the EPA over the long term, the scenarios are being used in policymaking situations. Frederick W. Talcott, who was involved from the beginning as the study's project officer, gives an example: "In a recent instance we were looking at a series of new incentives that would get private companies to come up with innovations in the area of pest control. We took three extreme scenarios from the study and applied the incentives to each one. The results were quite clear . . . Some buoyed up as they looked like they would work in all three scenarios while others wouldn't work in two out of three or all three." Other bureaus and departments in the Environmental Protection Agency are beginning to use the study for similar purposes, and copies have started to show up elsewhere in government.

In fact, it has begun to take on the proportions of an underground classic despite the fact that there has been no attempt to publicize it. Indeed, the same fears that have kept the FAA report from the Futures Group under wraps have caused the SRI study to be downplayed to the extreme that the agency's press office vetoed the idea of putting out a press release on the final report. Such announcements are the norm when a major study is completed, and, in fact, one was drafted for this one but quietly killed by the public information office, which got the jitters when it saw the ten scenarios. Talcott reports that despite this, requests for copies of the report pour in as word of it reaches other agencies of government, corporate planners, and individuals. More than 3,000 copies have been distributed through Talcott's office alone, which is remarkable for an intentionally unpublicized product of an obscure unit within a massive bureaucracy.

Obviously, the impact of the study has already gone beyond the EPA and will continue to do so, if only through excerpts and summaries such as what appears in this chapter. One reason why so much attention has been paid to this one particular study of the future is that, in the final analysis, its ten scenarios may have the greatest impact in individual terms—that is, they are so fascinating because they offer a realistic set of possibilities against which to measure the rest of our lives. They are quite different than those popular images of the future listed at the beginning of this chapter, but a lot more useful.

A second factor is suggested by Harman himself, who has been very pleased with the response to this particular study. "There are fundamental issues about the future which are not getting raised in a lot of studies because they come awfully close to being taboo. There are a lot of people both inside and outside government who want these issues raised and I think we did this in a respectable and plausible way."

THE STRAIGHT-UP SCENARIO

In January, 1976, three months after the EPA study was completed, the National Aeronautics and Space Administration released a futuristic study of its own called "Outlook for Space." It was the result of a gargantuán effort involving all sorts of working groups, study panels, polls, and outside research from such future-oriented institutions as the Hudson Institute, the Futures Group, and Forecasting International. The object of the study was to look at the projects the United States might wish to consider during the next twenty-five years in space.

In all, sixty-one specific objectives were listed in the final report, ranging from practical ones like gaining the ability to dispose of nuclear wastes in space to intellectual ones like determining the nature of black holes.

It would take many pages to outline all the possibilities discussed in the study, but the listing of a handful is in order.

• The establishment of the first large-scale solar power station in space before the year 2000. The station would collect and convert solar energy into electrical current in space and relay it to earth via a microwave system. This 20th-century prototype would pave the way for a significant number of solar stations in the first half of the 21st century, ultimately providing a large share of the earth's energy from space.

• The development of power relay satellites able to move huge amounts of power over long distances. Such a system, which could be operational by 1993, would permit energy to be flashed from remote locations to populated areas by "wireless" transmission. This means that solar power stations in the world's deserts, distant hydroelectric plants and nuclear power stations located in either unpopulated places on earth or in space could all become part of the system.

• Multiple efforts aimed at answering questions about the nature of the universe, the fate of matter, the life cycle of the stars, the evolution of the solar system, and the origins and future of life.* Answers provided from these scientific quests could ultimately provide unimagined benefits to the people on earth.

• Pre-2000 satellite-based systems for long-range climate (as opposed to simple weather) prediction, earthquake prediction, and the detection (and ultimately control) of the breeding grounds of harmful insects. There could also be other earth-oriented space systems ranging from those which would keep an active inventory of world resources (timber, water, crops, etc.) to stepped-up efforts to prospect for new energy and mineral sources on earth from clues picked up by satellites.

Beyond the matters discussed for the next twenty-five years, the "Outlook for Space" study looked at the potential significance of certain "big concepts" which were not given a date for starting or even suggested as bona fide projects at this point, but which *might* be undertaken—

---

* Some of the specific questions posed by NASA: How did the universe begin? What are quasars? What is the nature of gravity? Is there extraterrestrial life in the solar system? Can we detect extraterrestrial intelligent life? What is the ultimate fate of the sun? Do other stars have planets? Will the universe expand forever? How did the universe begin?

or at least initiated—by the turn of the century. Each of them will require much study and initial design in the near future.

One of these big, ambitious concepts is the exploitation of the moon from a permanent scientific and industrial base located there. (One possibility: there could be major savings in building massive space solar stations on the moon from material mined and processed on the spot.) Another is the creation of those oft-discussed space colonies which, among other things, could become industrial bases that would not pollute the earth's atmosphere. Pollutants would be blown away and dissipated in space by solar wind like the dust and gas from comet tails. Still another involves bringing iron-nickel asteroids back to earth to renew our supplies of those metals. Such a mission would be beyond the capacity of 20th-century technology but appears feasible for the 21st.

The importance of the NASA study is not just the sixty-one specific objectives and the further-out possibilities that it discusses, but its collective impact, which is that of still another alternative vision beyond the scope of the FAA or EPA scenarios, both of which are largely social and economic. NASA's "Outlook" (which is basically its own rough agenda) does not necessarily preclude any of those other scenarios from taking place, but could spawn all sorts of alternatives of its own.

6

TOMORROW'S TIMETABLE

A Year-by-Year Calendar of Events and Developments Forecast for the Period from 1980 to the Middle of the 21st Century

On July 4, 1976, the Bicentennial Day, the Boston *Sunday Globe* came out with an imaginative wrap-around section giving the news for the first Sunday in July, 2076. This Tricentennial edition is a fascinating example of forecasting peppered with such developments as the opening of the Ralph Nader Memorial Museum (located on part of the site of the old General Motors Corporation), the regeneration of an extinct European bison through the genetic manipulation of American bison stock, marriage contract insurance policies, and a protest march (led by William F. Buckley, 5th) calling for an end to world government and a return to nationalism and the free enterprise system. There is even an advice column in which a computer does what Ann Landers did in the 20th century, a classified ad section dealing with limbs and organs, a social note on the marriage of star Red Sox pitcher Barbara Botsford, and an episode of "Mutt and Jeff" in which the ever-hapless Jeff crashes to the ground after pushing the wrong button on his air transporter, causing him to say, "I'm starting the Fourth with a bang!"

For all of its fascinating touches, however, many of the technical developments forecast in this special edition of the *Globe* actually seem *conservative* when compared with what has been forecast in formal studies by government, research institutes, and industrial futures groups. The *Globe* talks about weather modification programs beginning in 2060, which is decades later than several large-scale Delphi studies have indicated such a development will take place; the imagined uses of lasers are trivial (such as using a laser knife to cut a wedding cake), and some of the new products talked about in the paper would probably be antiques or museum pieces in 2076. An example of the latter is a new hog of a car (a V-16 with twelve on the floor) which sounds like a dream of the 1950s gone wild. The paper also reports on a major tobacco raid in which enough raw materials to make 23 million illegal cigarettes are confiscated by officials. The implication is, of course, that cigarettes will have been totally banned by the 21st century for health reasons. However, several studies that have looked at trends in technology predict that safe, noncarcinogenic cigarettes will be developed and on the market by the 1980s. (If cigarettes are banned in the next century, a better guess for the reason for such an action is that the fertile land needed to produce tobacco will be needed for food.)

While the average American commonly comes in contact with quick predictions like those made by the *Globe*, few get to read the forecasts which have been obtained collectively at a cost of many millions of dollars (much of it from public funds) and with the help of thousands of consultants, experts, futurists, and the like. This is not because the bulk of these more formal studies are secret (although some are, and others are simply kept out of circulation by the military or private corporations), but because they normally do not show up in bookstores, are seldom publicized, and even if one is aware of, say, a government study on the future of medicine you must go through a fairly elaborate process of locating the document number and price before ordering it by mail from the appropriate office.

Even the seemingly routine matter of finding out what future studies have been done by the federal government can be a costly undertaking. The Commerce Department's National Technical Information Service will do a computerized search of studies with the word "future" in them for $100 (with no guarantee of how many will be found), and you would have to ante up another $100 if you wanted to hit the keyword "forecast." The Smithsonian will do a computer check on futures studies in progress for $50. Copies of many of the reports are in the $10 to $20 range and often take months to get after they have been ordered.

What is more, the reports themselves are often fat documents crammed with charts, formulas, and seemingly endless detail on methodology which one must wade through to find the actual predictions. With the exception of specialized magazines like *The Futurist* and *Futures*, the media pay little attention to them, and the sections of public libraries devoted to forecasting are usually dominated by Jeanne Dixon books.

SCHEDULING THE FUTURE

To cut through all of this for an idea of exactly what is being forecast, dozens of these reports—many based on Delphi studies—were collected, culled for specific predictions, summarized, and assembled here in calendar form.

Before beginning this master list, a few quick points are in order. In many cases, the predictions were created by panels of individuals whose estimates differed, so the years given are the median dates forecasted. Second, in most cases the forecast is based on the assumption that there is a 50 percent or better chance of the actual event taking place by that point in time—it is very hard to find an expert who believes that any specific forecast can be made with 100 percent surety. Third, I've picked these particular predictions as a *sampling* of what is being forecast, not a comprehensive list. To make it readable, very obvious forecasts and conflicting dates which came out of different studies have been left out. Fourth, since the samplings are from different studies, in a few places they may ostensibly contradict each other. Finally, it must be kept in mind that these predictions are made without considering "wild card" developments or intervention to prevent the event from taking place.

With that out of the way, here is the summary of the developments which government, industry, and the academic community have spent so much time and money predicting.*

1980

• One of ten colleges and universities in operation in 1975 has been forced to close or merge due to problems of finance and/or enrollment. (Consensus of a panel of educators assembled by the Carnegie Foundation for the Advancement of Teaching, 1975)

• The surplus of college graduates who are overqualified for the jobs available to them totals 140,000, more than a tenfold increase from the oversupply of the mid-1970s. Pressure is building to reduce the deficit in jobs available to recent college graduates. (U.S. Bureau of Labor Statistics, 1975)

• Colleges have begun working with the concept of the "video faculty exchange program," in which campuses are linked by television. (The Futures Group, report to the Electronics Industry Association, 1972)

• The development of teaching machines that are so sophisticated that they not only respond to the students' answers but to physiologic responses (tension, for instance) as well. (IFTF, 1969)

---

* Some major studies which are referenced more than a few times have been abbreviated as follows: The RAND Corporation's "Report on a Long-Range Forecasting Study" as "Rand, 1964," the Institute for the Future's "Forecasts of Some Technological and Scientific Developments and Their Societal Consequences" as "IFTF, 1969," NASA's "Outlook for Space" study as "NASA, 1976," NASA's "Outlook for Aeronautics" study as "NASA, Aeronautics, 1976," the U.S. Forest Service's "Future Leisure Environments" report as "Forest Service, 1974," Smith Kline and French Laboratories' "Delphic Study of the Future of Medicine" as "SKF, 1969," the International Red Cross and Sandoz, Ltd.'s "Health in 1980–1990" as "Red Cross/Sandoz, 1974," and various reports of the Trend Analysis Program as "TAP."

• The power of OPEC has deteriorated to the point that it is no longer able to control petroleum prices. (University of Southern California Center for Futures Research, 1976)

• Controlled underground nuclear explosions are used in the production of natural gas and oil. (Poll of energy experts, *The Futurist*, February, 1974)

• The nation is in the grips of a new crisis: the shortage of drinking water. (Producer's Council Delphi, 1974)

• Regular and reliable weather forecasts are given fourteen days in advance for areas as small as 100 square miles. (IFTF, 1969)

• A national system of economic incentives has come into being to encourage the conservation of fish and wildlife on private land. (Forest Service, 1974)

• The period of tough restriction on the use of the nation's wilderness and recreation lands has begun. Cans and glass containers have been banned from wilderness areas, the use of recreational vehicles restricted to roads only in public areas, and certain types of recreation are now restricted to certain seasons and time periods. (Forest Service, 1974)

• Working automated equipment for instant translation from one language to another is demonstrated. (IFTF, 1969)

• Cheap contraceptive agents are developed for mass administration, such as through water supplies. (IFTF, 1969)

• Facsimile systems for sending written or pictorial information over phone lines have more than tripled in number from the 100,000 systems on line in 1976. (Study by Creative Strategies, Inc., 1976)

• Public health agencies in the developed nations have begun routine prophylactic examinations of entire populations to catch diseases while they are still in a treatable state. (Red Cross/Sandoz, 1974)

• A true noncarcinogenic cigarette comes on the market. (SKF, 1969)

• A vaccine has been introduced to prevent serum hepatitis which will keep this disease under the same effective level of control as polio. (Red Cross/Sandoz, 1974)

• With a full 45 percent of all American wives employed outside the home, the trend to greater equality between husbands and wives is clearly established. Couples are increasingly sharing more powers and duties. (General Mills Corporation Planning Document, 1975)

• According to the latest figures, the cities which have grown the fastest in the last decade have been Dallas, Anaheim, San Jose, Miami, Atlanta, Houston, Denver, and the combined San Bernadino–Riverside area. One out of five Americans now moves every year. (The Futures Group, report to the Electronic Industries Association, 1972)

• The American economy is in good shape. The inflation rate, which was rising at a level of over 10 percent for 1974 and 1975, has now fallen to a much more comfortable 4 percent, and the unemployment rate is down from the 1975 peak of 9.2 percent to 5.5 percent. Energy prices are high but, due to recent tax cuts and a decreasing rate of inflation, the real disposable income of the average American is on the rise. Rail service has improved considerably and is far more popular than it was a few years ago. Americans are flying more, with 274 million tickets sold during the year for domestic air travel—an average of about one ticket per person. Reduced speed limits and gas prices have made the car a less competitive form of travel, especially for trips between cities linked by air or rail routes. ("Challenge of the Decade Ahead," Federal Aviation Administration, 1976)

1981–1985

• Two-way computer terminals for the home have become available and are beginning to offer a wide variety of services to the American home. (Unpublished IBM study cited in a report from the Futures Group, 1972)

1982

• The performing arts have priced themselves out of the market for all but well-to-do patrons. Federal and foundation grants can no longer bridge the gap between production costs and admission fees. Movie theaters are declining in number as pay cable TV and the use of home video tape machines grow. Magazine subscription prices have risen so sharply that fewer and fewer people can afford them. However, the use of public libraries has increased significantly. (*Florida 10 Million*, Florida Division of State Planning, 1973)

• Pilot programs in two-way electronic monitoring and consultation are allowing more and more people to get routine medical services in their homes without doctors having to leave their offices. The "house call" has returned to medicine, albeit electronically. (*Florida 10 Million*, 1973)

• Violent crime is rising and increasingly associated with younger age groups, population density, and increasing affluence. The areas that have grown the fastest in recent years are most vulnerable. (*Florida 10 Million*, 1973)

• Florida's population has just gone over the 10 million mark, making it the eighth largest state in population. The state entertains 40 million tourists a year (up 90 percent since 1970), and it has been urbanized to the point where 91 percent of its residents now live in densely populated areas mostly along the two coasts. Living costs in the state have reached an all-time high because of such factors as land costs, water shortages, increased costs of services, pollution control expenses, and the need to travel longer distances to find recreation areas. People are increasingly aware of "quality inflation," a term used to describe the higher prices paid for poorer quality workmanship and inferior materials. A growing share of the average family's income must now be earmarked for the repair or replacement of shoddy goods. (*Florida 10 Million*, 1973)

• The pay for so-called necessary work—garbage collection, dishwashing, domestic service—is commonly equivalent to that of white-collar employment. (*Florida 10 Million*, 1973)

1984

• A system for dumping hazardous nuclear wastes in space is tested. The spacecraft is automated, "abortproof," and capable of getting rid of a half-ton load of waste out of the earth's atmosphere. (NASA, 1976)

1985

• In terms of Gross National Product, here is a rough picture of how the world's major nations are faring:

$2,000 Billion—the United States

$1,000 Billion—Japan and the USSR

$500 Billion—France and West Germany

$250 Billion—China, Canada, Italy, and the United Kingdom

$120 Billion—Brazil, India, Mexico, East Germany, and Poland

$60 Billion—The Netherlands, Sweden, Belgium, Australia, Iran, Argentina, Switzerland, and Indonesia

(NASA, Aeronautics, 1976)

• The size of the U.S. federal, state, and local governments continues to increase, with approximately one out of every six workers employed by some form of government—a far cry from 1900, when only one in twenty-four was on a government payroll. (Futuremics, 1975)

• There is a major oversupply of PhDs in America, with more than 135,000 unable to come up with jobs equal to their level of education. The greatest surplus is among those with doctorates in the social sciences. (The figure is the average of two bleak 1976 projections, one made by the National Science Foundation, the other by the Bureau of Labor Statistics.)

• There have been some interesting changes in the character of the American population. More than half the workforce hold white collar jobs for the first time in history. Education levels have climbed to the point that 70 percent of the population has at least a high school diploma, a far cry from 1960, when only 41 percent had finished high school. A record number of households—a shade below a quarter of the total—are occupied by a single person. There are nearly two women for each man in this single-household group because of the growing predominance of widows over widowers. In terms of consumer behavior, the average American prefers quality to quantity, natural over artificial, and durability over disposability. There is little tolerance for conspicuous waste. (Institute for the Future report to Corporate Associates, 1975)

• The employee benefits that are the norm for the American worker have reached the level at which 50 percent of payroll costs go into benefits. Flexible working hours are common and the work week is almost universally set at thirty-five hours. The number of paid holidays and vacation days has risen markedly in recent years, and companies offer more and more leisure-oriented benefits— ranging from free theater tickets to the use of company-owned recreation areas—as a matter of course. There are many free or heavily subsidized educational opportunities that come with a job, including paid sabbaticals for job-related study. Medical insurance programs are all-inclusive and companies offer group automobile and homeowner's liability insurance. Employees have considerable freedom in tailoring individual packages of benefits to their own needs, and most companies now have "benefit counselors" to help. ("A Study of Potential Changes in Employee Benefits," Institute for the Future, 1969)

• The United States has passed through the first phase of the energy crisis which began in the 1970s. Great emphasis has been put on conservation (a combination of rising prices and appeals made in the public interest), reduced oil imports, and the exploitation of existing technology. The nation is now entering the second phase of the crisis, during which it will attempt to become energy self-sufficient, a quest that is expected to take at least twenty-five years to accomplish. ("Some Societal Impacts of Alternative Energy Policies," Institute for the Future, 1975)

• A full quarter of American electricity now comes from nuclear power plants. (University of Southern California, Center for Futures Research, 1976)

(At this point it is interesting to include a probability which came out of a Delphi exercise at the University of Southern California Center for Futures Research in 1976 which says that there is a 70 percent chance of another oil embargo before 1985 and an 80 percent chance of another Arab-Israeli war.)

• Aircraft noise levels have been reduced from those of the mid-1970s by approximately 80 percent, substantially solving the air noise problem and making airports more acceptable to their neighboring communities. ("Challenge of the Decade Ahead," Federal Aviation Administration, 1976)

• The need for recreational land has become such that the government has begun offering financial incentives to private landowners who open their lands to the public. (Forest Service, 1974)

• Drugs which control human pigmentation have been invented. (SKF, 1969)

• The need to diet to lose weight has become a thing of the past, as all food stores stock special foods and food supplements which control a person's weight. (IFTF, 1974)

• A synthetic blood substitute has been developed and is now being tested. (SKF, 1969)

• Means have been discovered for the electrical control of pain, and the "electronic anesthetic" is now coming into use in hospitals. (The Futures Group, report to the Electronics Industry Association, 1972)

• About 30 percent of all American medical students are now women, compared with 18 percent ten years earlier. (Association of American Medical Colleges study, 1975)

• An artificial colon has been developed. (SKF, 1969)

• Life expectancy for the average American has now reached the seventy-five-year mark. Many more people are choosing optional retirement at age fifty-five. (IFTF, 1974)

• Record amounts of money are being spent on body care, with the bulk of it going for lotions, creams, plastic surgery, and weight control supplements. (IFTF, 1974)

• The national crime rate has doubled in the last decade with predictable results: people are generally more fearful and fewer friendships are based on informal neighborhood contacts. (IFTF, 1974)

• In recent years there has been a home television "information explosion" because of advances in cable systems, video recording, and computer applications. It has now reached the level that subscribers are able to contract for such in-home television services as these:

- adult evening courses
- banking services
- special sales information
- daily calendar and reminder about appointments
- secretarial assistance
- computer-aided instruction
- message recording
- consumer's advisory service
- access to company files
- legal information
- grocery price lists, information and the ability to order
- bus, train, and air scheduling
- answering services
- special sale information
- credit card transactions
- ticket reservation services
- correspondence schools
- access to company files
- library access

(IFTF, 1970)

1985–1988

- Chemical control over senility has become a reality. (*Technological Breakthroughs and Widespread Application of Significant Technical Developments*, McGraw-Hill Economics Department, 1973)

1986
- The number of employed Americans is now over 100 million—104 million to be exact—and, despite continually rising fuel costs, new car sales are only slightly below 10 million a year. ("Challenge of the Decade Ahead," Federal Aviation Administration, 1976)

1988
- A number of coal mines have become fully automated with no humans having to work underground. (Poll of energy experts, *The Futurist*, February, 1974)

1989
- Artificial hands with a sense of touch and maneuverability close to those of human hands have been developed.

(Science and Technology Agency of the Japanese Government, 1971)

• Self-repairing computers have become a reality. These units can locate, diagnose, and fix most malfunctions and breakdowns without human intervention. (Science and Technology Agency of the Japanese Government, 1971)

1990

• The malpractice concept has spread to all the professions with some unpleasant results including professional strikes and periods in which services are withheld. (Institute of Life Insurance Trend Analysis Program report, "Culture in Transformation," 1975)

• Public confidence in political, educational, religious, labor, and corporate institutions has been steadily declining since the Watergate period of the 1970s. These institutions and their leaders no longer fit in with America's new goals, life styles, and attitudes. Meanwhile, many of the old divisions—local/global, public/private, conservative/liberal—have become significantly blurred. (Institute of Life Insurance Trend Analysis Program report, "Culture in Transformation," 1975)

• Legislation is passed in the United States establishing the petroleum industry as a public utility (or it is nationalized altogether). (University of Southern California Center for Futures Research, 1976)

• Most American homes have at least one videotape system. (Forest Service, 1974)

• Rigid new transportation legislation has banned private aircraft from metropolitan airports and only permits non-polluting vehicles in downtown areas. (Forest Service, 1974)

• American public schools are operating on a year-round schedule with vacations staggered throughout the year. (Forest Service, 1974)

• The American consumer has learned to accept the costs of pollution control which are major, and it is now the norm for the government to close any company that does not comply with pollution standards. That nation relies on a nationwide pollution monitoring system for the quick detection of violators. (Forest Service, 1974)

• Pressures on the use of outdoor recreation and National Park land have led to the common use of wear-resistant hiking paths, electronic guide systems, and restrictive fences. Camping in public areas is now controlled by a national computerized reservation system. The power of recreational boat engines has been restricted by law, and salt-water fishing requires a federal license. (Forest Service, 1974)

• Skiing has developed into an all-year sport due to the development and widespread use of artificial surfaces. (Forest Service, 1974)

• Heart, lung, and liver transplants are commonplace, and doctors now perform new types of grafts beyond the common skin graft, including teeth and blood vessels. It is also possible to replace damaged nerves and nerve channels in the spinal cord. In fact, save for the brain itself and the spinal cord, anything can be replaced by transplants or man-made artificial devices. (Red Cross/Sandoz, 1974)

• Artificial "eyesight" for the blind is widely available due to developments in electronic sensors. (*Technological Breakthroughs and Widespread Application of Significant Technical Developments*, McGraw-Hill Economics Department, 1973)

• Although there have been many advances in genetic engineering in recent years, the idea of preventing inherited diseases is still a dream of the future. However, knowledge has progressed to the point where these possibilities can be predicted with greater surety in advance. (Red Cross/Sandoz, 1974)

• The growing costs of health care in most nations are largely handled through tax-supported national health services or obligatory national health insurance plans. (Red Cross/Sandoz, 1974)

• The per capita consumption of pharmaceutical products has doubled from its 1970 level. (Red Cross/Sandoz, 1974)

• There is mass screening of populations for diseases not only to locate early evidence of them but also to identify predisposing factors. (Red Cross/Sandoz, 1974)

• Vaccines first introduced in the 1980s have effectively rid the world of venereal diseases. (Red Cross/Sandoz, 1974)

• Cancer is still a major disease, but because of major advances in its detection, prevention, and treatment, 70 percent of all cancers are now generally controllable. Surgery for tumors has become obsolete, as they are now chemically treated. (Red Cross/Sandoz, 1974)

• Chemical therapy for the control of certain psychoses has become common; virtually all types of neuroses are treatable and some can actually be cured. (Red Cross/Sandoz, 1974)

• So-called social drugs have reached a new level of sophistication and variety. New energizers, tranquilizers, stimulants, and euphoriants are very effective and specific in what they can do. Other drugs are available to stimulate sexuality, treat alcoholism, reduce obesity, and end dependence on other drugs. There are male oral contraceptives and pills to induce abortion at an early stage. (Red Cross/Sandoz, 1974)

• The United States has almost twice the number of physicians it had in 1970, with the result that there is now one doctor for every 422 citizens as opposed to the 1970 rate of 1:630. (Health, Education and Welfare report, *The Supply of Health Manpower*, 1974)

• There is a complete understanding of the psychologic and physiologic causes of human depression. (SKF, 1969)

1991

• The age of the robot sporting event has dawned with the commercial availability of mechanical humans for violent contact sports. (Science and Technology Agency of the Japanese Government, 1971)

1991–1992

• A multiton spacecraft returns from Mars with a kilogram sample of Martian soil. The vehicle has orbited outside the earth's atmosphere for some time in biological quarantine. (NASA, 1976)

1992

• 3-D television comes into routine use. (IFTF, 1969)
• Complex "household" robots are available which can perform a number of domestic jobs including housecleaning and the preparation of meals. (IFTF, 1969)
• Means are discovered to safely reduce the amount of sleep required. (IFTF, 1969)
• Drugs are available to heighten the perception of normal people and increase the learning speed of the retarded. (IFTF, 1969)
• The political map of America continues to change with the "Sunbelt" ascending in power. For this year's presidential election that part of the nation has sixteen more electoral votes (and sixteen more members of the House) than it did in the 1976 election. Florida with eight more electors and Texas with three are the big winners, while New York has lost four, Pennsylvania three, and Illinois and Ohio are each down two. (National Planning Association, 1976)

1994

• Methods have been developed for predicting earthquakes with great reliability up to one month in advance for areas as small as 1,000 square miles. (Science and Technology Agency of the Japanese Government, 1971)

1995

• The once-small "nuclear club" has become a major organization with a membership roster that includes Taiwan, Argentina, Brazil, South Africa, Israel, Egypt, Pakistan, and Iran. Evidence has come to light that strongly suggests that at least one international terrorist group has also slipped into the club. The United States and other developed nations are spending vast sums on systems for detecting the clandestine movement of A-bombs and potential nuclear extortionists. (NASA, Aeronautics, 1976)
• The business and professional world has changed considerably. Some of its new characteristics include: varying retirement age with no upper limit, widespread use of paraprofessionals and apprentices, many more people work-

ing at home, worker representation on corporate boards of directors, increased job mobility (both within and between organizations), and a general breakdown of the old hierarchical structure, with workers now in possession of greater decision-making powers. (TAP report, 1975)

• American communities display a mixture of old and new ideas. A tour of the nation would reveal many examples of communities with enforced limits on future growth, a number of "grow our own" areas in which agriculture has been brought back into the community, and many places where cable TV and computer terminals are used to link individual houses into local policymaking and information networks. There is a new generation of "new" towns and cities, and new life has been given to some of the older cities through effective redevelopment. (TAP report, 1975)

• The traditional political molds are breaking down as the number of "new breed" political leaders continues to grow —especially at the state and local level. They are interested in building new institutions and rely on new styles of decision-making. They baffle traditional politicians with their mix of liberal and conservative attitudes. They seem to appreciate power but use it with restraint and have been typified by their ability to combine "Eastern ideology with Western tactics." (TAP report, 1975)

• The national pollution index has fallen to its lowest level in many decades. The average is now 10 percent on a scale in which zero equals no pollution and 100 percent means the extinction of life. In contrast, the level was at 25 percent in 1975 and 20 percent in 1985. (University of Southern California Center for Futures Research, 1976)

• China's population is just over a billion, making it the first nation in history to achieve this size. India, however, is close behind and will soon join the billion-people club. (United Nations Population Division, 1975)

• Two major new forms of commercial aircraft have come on the market with each bidding to have a major impact on air travel. The first is a very quiet VTOL (for Vertical Takeoff and Landing) aircraft that can operate from very small landing sites. It has been nicknamed the

"Downtowner" because a number of them can operate from urban airports as the nuclei for new efforts to revitalize the cities. The VTOLs will be used primarily for linking passengers to new "hub" airports which are centers for long-haul travel and for fast shuttles to other cities in the region.

The other big announcement in aviation is the first flight of the Advanced Supersonic Transports, which allow intercontinental travel to distances of 6,000 to 8,000 miles within four hours or less. These planes are quieter, cheaper, and more efficient in the use of fuel, and give a "better ride" than the first SSTs which came into use in the 1970s.

• People in the aviation industry feel that the Advanced SST will lead to the ultimate development of hydrogen-fueled hypersonic transports after the year 2000. It is believed that the hypersonic planes will operate from man-made islands twenty to thirty miles offshore where noise will be of little concern and hydrogen fuel will be produced on the spot from seawater. (NASA, Aeronautics, 1976)

• All commercial products in the United States are packaged in nonpolluting containers. (Forest Service, 1974)

• Suspended animation for humans is coming into widespread use during the administration of certain medical treatments like complicated operations. (SKF, 1969)

• Medical diagnosis has become a largely automated process seldom involving MDs. For instance, the annual physical has become a series of chemical and electronic tests which the patient administers to himself or herself at various stations. (SKF, 1969)

1998

• Based on experiments which began in the early 1980s, a satellite system is now in operation that provides solar power relayed from space. The first space power station on earth is in operation. (NASA, 1976)

1998–1999

• An operational satellite system collects the information needed for reliable earthquake prediction from space. (NASA, 1976)

1999

• The ability to regulate the possession of nuclear weapons in the world is no better now than the ability to regulate the possession of heroin or Saturday-night specials was in the 1970s. (Consensus of a panel of arms control experts who also agreed that some nuclear wars were likely to have occurred before 2000, *Harvard Magazine*, 1975)

2000

• As the world's leaders look back on the last twenty-five years since the long war in Southeast Asia, they term it a period of "No major war—no major peace." The superpowers have maintained their power without resorting to nuclear conflict, but there have been numerous small wars as the developing nations experienced growing pains. (NASA, Aeronautics, 1976)*

• Some 700,000 pounds of plutonium and weapons-grade uranium are moving through the civilian economy of the United States each year—enough to make 17,000 weapons of the size that leveled Hiroshima fifty-five years ago. (Conclusion from a series of thirty-one studies made for the U.S. Nuclear Regulatory Agency on the matter of nuclear terrorism and sabotage, 1976)

• Lasers are coming into use for "wireless" power transmission. (Poll of energy experts, *The Futurist*, February, 1974)

• Nuclear electric spacecraft (unmanned) launched in 1997 successfully intercepted an asteroid in 1998 and has returned a one-kilogram asteroid sample. (NASA, 1976)

• The world's population is 7 billion, up 3 billion from twenty-five years earlier. (NASA, 1976—based on the assumption of constant fertility and no global disasters)

• The situation in India is extremely grim. The population, which has more than doubled in the last twenty-five years, has just hit 960 million and should soon go over a billion. Meanwhile, these same twenty-five years have seen the per capita availability of food decline by a third. The

---

* There is some contradiction between this and the previous forecast, indicating the variety of forecasts in matters of war and peace.

housing crisis is so severe that the government estimates that $60 million will be required to solve the problem. Power is scarce and a coal shortage is imminent. (A draft paper on the national future from the Indian National Committee on Science and Technology, 1975. Predictions are based on what will happen if there is no radical turnaround in agriculture, energy, and birth control.)

• More than 200 cities in the Third World have more than a million residents, in dramatic contrast with the 60 cities of that size in the lesser-developed world of 1976. (United Nations, International Labor Organization, 1976)

• International superagencies are in operation halting air and water pollution worldwide and containing accidental oil spills and other open sea pollution. In the United States only safe, biodegradable chemicals are allowed to be discharged directly into the environment. (Forest Service, 1974)

• Because of the reduced birthrate and improved health care, the U.S. population (about 290 million) has aged significantly. A full third of the population is over forty-five (as compared with 1975, when less than a quarter of the population was over forty-five). (NASA, 1976)

• The United States government has begun use of tax incentives to control population growth. (Forest Service, 1974)

• Specific areas of the nation have declined substantially in population. Hardest hit are the old seaports (especially the shallower ones which cannot handle the deep-draft superships), coal and iron mining regions, the "black belt" in the Deep South, and the Great Plains. This has been brought about by new methods and technology in shipping, farming, and mining which require much less labor. In the Great Plains, for instance, productive farming requires fewer and fewer farmers and farm workers each year, and it is now an ironic fact that most of the nation's "agricultural workers" can be found in factories producing fertilizer and new machinery. There has been a major revival in coal mining and the industry is far more mechanized and capital-intensive than ever before. (NASA, Aeronautics, 1976)

• In contrast to the 1970s, urban areas have grown significantly, having consumed new land areas equivalent in size to New Hampshire, Vermont, Massachusetts, and Rhode Island combined. Urban America is now a full one third of the nation in size, which has caused difficult problems in regard to wildland and wildlife preservation, recreation, and croplands. (NASA, 1976)

• In fact, more than half the American population (54 percent) lives in two giant urban sectors: 13 percent of the total population resides along the coastal strip between San Diego and San Francisco and 41 percent lives in the "metropolitan belt" stretching along the northern Atlantic seaboard and westward to Chicago. (Population and the American Future, 1972)

• Since more than 80 percent of the U.S. population lives in urban areas, the trends set earlier toward congestion, crime, pollution, and the alienation of the individual have continued. (NASA, 1976)

• Blacks and other nonwhites comprise 40 percent of the nation's center cities, which is up from the average of 22 percent back in the mid-20th century, when the Kerner Commission envisioned "two societies" for America, one black, one white. The inner cities and the depopulating rural areas have both suffered from the flow of jobs to the suburbs and, more than ever, are characterized by people with low skills and poor education, deteriorating and abandoned housing, and poor public facilities. (Population and the American Future, 1972)

• Water has become an increasingly precious commodity, with more and more of the nation coping with constant shortages. Agriculture, industry, and the public have learned to conserve water. There is still enough water for drinking and other essentials, but lawn-watering has gone the way of leaf burning as an outdoor activity. (Population and the American Future, 1972)

• The average retirement age for the American worker is now forty-seven, which promises an individual twenty-five to thirty-five years in retirement. The position of the older worker is now diminished with a mere 10 percent of the work-force working past age sixty-five as compared with twenty-five percent back in 1975. (Futuremics, 1975)

• One statistic that is the source of growing national concern is the ratio of widows to widowers, which has increased over the last quarter century from 4 to 1 to a stunning 6 to 1. (Futuremics, 1975)

• The United States is consuming the equivalent of 80 to 120 million barrels of oil per day as contrasted with the daily use of 30 million barrels in the mid-1970s. Most reliable estimates now predict that all oil and natural gas deposits will be depleted during the 21st century. (NASA, 1976)

• Compared to the early 1970s, the income of the average American has nearly doubled and the hours for leisure have increased significantly. This has put great strain on outdoor recreation, as the same urge that commonly turned Yosemite National Park into a weekend city with a population of 50,000 in the 1970s has had to be brought under control. Access to the great outdoors requires a permit which must be applied for in advance. (Population and the American Future, 1972)

• The urban recreation picture has changed as well. In order to get more play area, cemeteries and reservoirs are being opened as public recreation facilities, and some parks are now enclosed so they can be used under any weather conditions. Artificial turf is used in most public areas where sports are played and there are even some artificially surfaced golf courses. In some urban areas, there are indoor recreation centers which simulate natural outdoor environments. (Forest Service, 1974)

• Both the structure of leisure and public attitude toward it have changed profoundly. "Weekends" are now flexible and distributed throughout the week to reduce the pressure on recreational facilities, and a "reasonable" one-way distance for a family to travel on a weekend is 500 miles. The government grants tax breaks to those companies that incorporate recreational areas into their new plant designs, and the role of public schools includes providing recreational opportunities to the entire community. National Park and wilderness areas are protected with the aid of tough regulations and new technology. Electronic sensors monitor parks, "waste-eating" bacteria units are mandatory for recreational equipment, and wildlife migrations are checked by earth-orbiting satellites. Endangered species are bred in captivity and then released into the wild, and the main "use" of wildlife has shifted from hunting, now highly restricted, to watching and photographing. (Forest Service, 1974)

• Use of modifiers (brain surgery or psychochemicals) to change criminal behavior is widespread. (IFTF, 1969)

• The ability of certain drugs to permanently raise the level of human intelligence is proven. (IFTF, 1969)

• The behavior of elements of society is controlled by radio stimulation of the brain. (IFTF, 1969)

• "Human cloning" is a reality. This will allow one human to create his or her identical twin by having a somatic cell deposited in the ovum of a "host mother." (IFTF, 1969)

2001

• An unmanned spacecraft, launched in 1999, returns from Mercury with a kilogram sample of surface soil. (NASA, 1976)

2005

• Remote facsimile newspapers and magazines are printed in the home. (RAND, 1964)

2010

• Drugs have been introduced that can cure or prevent mental retardation. (SKF, 1969)

• The second phase of the energy crisis, which began in 1985, has finally ended. America is now self-sufficient in regard to energy but consuming the last of its oil and natural gas deposits . . . and using up more and more coal to produce synthetic oil and gas. The recent years have been much like the 1970s in that there is great anxiety about the ability to develop new forms of energy to the level at which shortages are permanently ended. The United States is now entering the third stage of the crisis, in which new sources (solar, nuclear, and geothermal) take over. One problem of immense importance is finding suitable ways to store these new kinds of energy, which lack the easy handling of oil, coal, and gasoline. Meanwhile, America's new self-sufficiency has eased the situation somewhat in Japan and Europe because it is no longer competing for energy imports. ("Some Societal Impacts of Alternative Energy Policies," Institute for the Future, 1975)

2012
• "Fish farming" on both natural and man-made lakes and ponds has reached the point where it supplies one tenth of the world's food calories. (IFTF, 1969)

2015
• Replacement organs for humans are grown and harvested from specially bred animals. (*The Post-Physician Era: Medicine in the 21st Century*, 1976)
• Biochemical processes capable of stimulating the growth of new organs and limbs are discovered. (IFTF, 1969)

2020
• Because of the dwindling supply of open recreational land, man-made islands are being constructed for recreational use. (Forest Service, 1974)
• The successful breeding of intelligent animals, such as apes, is done for low-grade labor and ground-combat tasks. (RAND, 1964)

2024
• There are international agreements which guarantee minimum income levels to the world's population. This would be brought about by ever-increasing industrial productivity through automation and would be seen as a force that removes pressures that lead to war. (RAND, 1964)
• Two new space activities are being initiated: extraterrestrial farming and regularly scheduled commercial traffic to the lunar colony. (RAND, 1964)
• It is possible to keep a human brain alive outside the body for periods of, say, a month. (IFTF, 1969)

2025
- Proof is established that there are intelligent beings beyond the earth. (IFTF, 1969)

2030
- Most middle-income American families now own their own vacation homes. (Forest Service, 1974)

2050
- "Camping" is still very popular in America and is now commonly available in multistory buildings similar to the parking garages of the 20th century. (Forest Service, 1974)
- The United States has officially designated "the last acre" of wilderness land available for protection. It is commonly assumed that in the near future land pressures will become so great that areas will have to be withdrawn from wilderness status and developed. (Forest Service, 1974)

2063
- The ability to control gravity by some technique for changing an area's gravitational field has been mastered. In military terms, this would bring about such developments as "weightless" combat vehicles and the ability to raise enemy forces off the ground. (RAND, 1964)

After 2050
- Most American lakes and rivers are cleaned to the point where they support the variety of aquatic life that existed in 1800. (Forest Service, 1974)
- Hovercraft and jet-powered backpacks are in common recreational use by middle-class Americans. (Forest Service, 1974)
- Man-made rivers are constructed for strictly recreational uses. (Forest Service, 1974)
- The average American enters the workforce at age twenty-five, enjoys a three-month annual vacation, and can expect to live to be one hundred. The United States has mandatory population control. (Forest Service, 1974)
- For those without their own vacation homes, apartment

units are so designed that they can be detached and moved to recreational areas during the vacation period. (Forest Service, 1974)

Nevers, Unknowns, and Ifs

• In these studies there are often developments and events that are looked at but which get sorted into categories other than median dates for the simple reason that they are unknown, highly conditioned, or are never expected to take place. These are often as interesting as those forecasts which are given with dates, especially those which the experts do not expect ever to take place. Here is a sampling from these other categories:

Never

• Housing manufacturers begin marketing a "disposable home" with a maximum design life of no more than fifteen years. (Producer's Council Delphi, 1974)

• There is complete electronic or chemical control of human behavior. (SKF, "Delphic Study of the Future of Medicine, 1969)

• The reliable use of extrasensory perception as a form of communication is perfected. (IFTF, 1969) (This was actually rated at a split between "later than 2025" and "Never.")

• The fact that most humans have the capacity for genius which is not realized for reasons of motivation or "cultural receptivity" is proven. (IFTF, 1969)

• Oil or natural gas reemerges as the most available and least costly fuel for home heating. (Producer's Council Delphi, 1974)

• Because of changing life styles, more than 5 percent of the American population live in communes. (Producer's Council Delphi, 1974)

• Mass-hypnotic recruitment of forces from an enemy population is realized. (RAND, 1964)

• Domesticated porpoises or dolphins are used for anti-submarine reconnaissance. (RAND, 1964)

• Compulsory genetic manipulation is initiated to improve the quality of the human race. (Forest Service, 1974)

• Transparent roofs or bubbles cover most American cities. (Forest Service, 1974)
• An embargo is placed on all future American highway construction. (Forest Service, 1974)
• Radiation immunization is possible (through pills or other means). (RAND, 1964)
• Political boundaries are realigned to coincide with natural ecological boundaries. (Forest Service, 1974)

If
• If unlawful immigration into the United States is allowed to stay at the mid-1970s level, illegal aliens and their children will add at least 25 million to the population by the year 2000. (National Growth and Development Report, Department of Housing and Urban Development, 1976)

Unknown
• Manned flight to Mars. This will require an unknown period of research and development coupled with the will, national or international, and massive funding. Rated highly improbable for this century. (NASA, 1976)

BEYOND THE FORECASTS

While individual items in this collection of forecasts are interesting in themselves, they tend to become even more interesting when their possible implications are thought about, which is one of the main reasons they were worked up in the first place.

An example that has already attracted more than a little thought is the forecast of the Institute for the Future to the effect that there will be "nonsurgical techniques by which the sex of babies may be chosen with 90 percent certainty" by the year 1980. When that prediction was made, the panel that forecast it rated its impact as one that would be "detrimental" (on the scale of values that ranged from "very favorable" to "very detrimental") because it could lead to fads for sexes and major changes in sex roles. Others have talked about such possibilities as creating

great sexual imbalances in various segments of society—
for example, farm families will have mostly boy babies,
based on the conventional belief that males are more likely
to keep a farm operating than females.

A recent editorial in *Futures* magazine, aptly entitled
"A Man's World?", suggests another possibility with stag-
gering implications. The magazine says that this ability to
choose a child's sex coupled with the traditional preference
for males in underdeveloped nations like India might lead
to laws which read, "A woman may have as many sons as
she likes, but only one daughter." Overpopulated nations
might grab at this because it would limit population by
allowing fewer bearers of children—or, putting it in terms
of demographic law: the net reproduction rate is the rate
at which generations of women replace each other. If the
absolute goal is that of limiting population growth, this
solution could be tempting, but the developments that
could follow imply jarring social changes, ranging from the
need for massive standing armies to absorb the excess
males—something that could encourage new wars—to
states in which male homosexuality becomes an expression
of patriotism.

If we believe this prediction can come true, we must now
prepare for it and decide how it will be handled when the
discovery is made. Significantly, the group that made the
original forecast thinks that there is a fairly good chance
that its detrimental effects can be controlled through such
actions as financial reward systems to maintain an equal
sex ratio, legislation to regulate sex ratio and family size,
and public education programs. There is still another possibility not mentioned in the original study: attempting to
stop or slow this Pandora's box discovery.

Going further with some of the other developments that
we have just seen forecast, here are some other consequences which have occurred to those who have predicted
and then reflected on them.

Development	*Possible Consequence*
Chemical control of human aging	The use of this ability to reward elites—high-ranking

Development	Possible Consequence
	government officials, Senators, chemical company executives, etc.
Drugs able to produce specific personality changes	The emergence of a "supersoldier" under total emotional control
Development of mass-administrated contraceptive agents	A new form of warfare, contraceptive warfare—perhaps the ultimate weapon . . . and/or significant reduction of population pressures in underdeveloped and overpopulated nations
Perfection of organ transplant technology through solution of the "rejection" problem	Organ black markets; people being murdered for organs
Strict government control over wilderness areas	A new criminal class of hunters, fishermen, and snowmobilers
Proven genetic control techniques	Greater class differences based on the ability to pay for genetic services . . . and/or the "engineering" of specialized classes of people ranging from menials to those with physical and mental superpowers
Regular and reliable weather forecasts fourteen days in advance	Complications for the tourist industry as people only book their vacations for periods of good weather
Development of the human clone	Replication of great and essential people (top inventors, highly regarded artists, etc.)—resulting in a kind of immortality for some

Development	Possible Consequence
Lasers come into use for "wireless power transmission"	New hazards to flying objects ranging from commercial airliners to migrating birds
World population of 6 billion	Tremendous pressures on world agriculture including those to end all production which does not supply human nutrition. Tobacco, liquor, marijuana, and pet food could be viewed increasingly as "immoral" uses of land
A world that is virtually free of venereal diseases	Increasingly permissive and promiscuous societies
The ability to predict genetic diseases and detect carriers	The concept of a "genetic identity card," the possibility of illegal marriages, and the question of sterilization for genetic reasons—all likely to stir up tremendous debate
Wholesale increase in the variety, use, and availability of "social" drugs	Drug-induced mental disorders leading to the vicious circle requiring more drugs and/or wide-scale social manipulation as portions of the society are energized (factory workers) or tranquilized (the aged, the young) to make society more efficient
Heightened experimentation in the area of genetic control and engineering	Major mishaps as attempts are made to apply this technology—paralleling the thalidomide tragedy
Availability of a computer which understands standard	Self-replicating computers and advanced computers

Development	Possible Consequence
IQ tests and scores above 150	designed by other computers . . . and/or the raising of deep questions regarding human significance
The ability to maintain the human brain outside the body for periods up to a month	The exploration of environments hostile to humans (the brain could be enclosed in special armor for such adventures)

In some cases long lists of possibilities and probabilities can be generated from a single event. When, for instance, the Institute for the Future looked at the implications of the "feasibility of limited weather control in the sense of predictably affecting regional weather at acceptable cost," it listed these nine potential consequences:

1. Great improvements in agricultural efficiency by creating rain on demand, avoidance of floods, and minimizing the number of clouds over farms during sunlight hours. (Probable)
2. Disruption in ecological balance leading to the extinction of some plant and animal species. (Possible)
3. Weather being used as a military or economic weapon. (Probable)
4. Great increase in the number of civil suits alleging damage caused by weather manipulation. (Probable)
5. Emergence of a new power elite: "the weather makers." (Possible)
6. Unpredictable psychoses in the population.* (Possible)
7. International treaties and regulations concerning potential weather effects which cross national boundaries. (Virtually certain)
8. Unexpected and perhaps detrimental effects on certain aspects of the local, regional, or planetary weather. (Probable)

---

* Presumably mental illness could result as people lost faith in weather as a natural phenomenon.

9. Certain areas of the oceans becoming hurricane dissipation areas. (Possible)

Nor is it hard to imagine other possibilities: good
weather going to the highest bidder (pitting, say, Miami
against St. Petersburg), nations becoming increasingly
hostile to one another on the allegation that one has stolen
needed rain from another, man-made weather accidents
in which many are killed, technologically adept terrorists
using weather as a threat, and strong animosity between
interest groups as the farmers of an area want some August
rain and the resort owners of the same area don't want
any. This is to say nothing of some of the lesser impacts,
such as new forms of insurance, a new legal specialty, a
new regulatory agency, and a gaggle of new meteorological
lobbyists in Washington.

In cases like weather modification it is relatively easy to
see some of the major possibilties, but in others it takes
extra thought and imagination to see what might result.
For instance, at first glance it would seem that the development of computers able to translate immediately from one
language to another would be a favorable development,
especially in terms of crisis communications and the transfer of scientific and technical information. But when the
Institute for the Future looked at that development, one
of the consequences it listed as a probable outcome was
that of further ethnic separation between nations speaking
different languages. The reasoning behind this prediction
was that there would be fewer linguists after the computers began to take over and that this would lead to a less
intimate understanding of vocabulary nuances.

Special consideration must be made for those cases in
which two or more groups have predicted the same development and then give different interpretations to its
consequences. Often these differences are relatively slight,
but sometimes they are diametrically opposed. In looking
at the development of short-takeoff commercial aircraft in
its "Outlook for Aeronautics" study, NASA says that this
will help bring new vitality to the cities with new, small

in-town airports, but others have looked at the same development and held that they will create suburban mini-airports and sap urban commerce. While it might seem that such differences of opinion point to a weakness in forecasting, they can actually be seen as strengths because they serve to warn of areas where a great deal more thought has to be given to the impact of the event in question.

Significantly, there is growing evidence that such forecasts and their envisioned implications have been useful in getting policymakers to take a closer look at future events. Using just the example of weather modification, there are a number of major studies in progress which probe the effect of that technology, including several now being sponsored by the National Science Foundation. Such forecasts have also been catalysts in getting Congress to set up its Office of Technology Assessment and in getting the new "foresight" provision into law. Presumably, some of the forecasts we have just seen will be changed as their effects are better understood and intervention takes place.

There is another useful side to these predictions which is to help us examine our own personal futures. The most convenient way to put these things into a context is to assemble them in scenario form to see how a situation might shape up. One group that has been working with the idea of the personal scenario is the Institute of Life Insurance's Trend Analysis Program, which has basically used other people's forecasts to create such scripts as one on the life cycles of one John Smith (born to a single mother in Chicago in 1985 and dying of sudden lung failure in 2070 while teaching comparative architecture), and another on the electronically dominated life of an insurance salesman in the year 1990. (Both of these appear in a later section of Bonus Scenarios.) Among the group's more interesting exercises of this type is one based on various predictions on the future of employment to chart the events following the hiring of a person for a new job in the mid-1980s. Here is an adaptation of that scenario presented to show how personal scenarios are created.

HIRED IN 1985

You are hired by a company at a total compensation of $23,000 which is to include your salary and benefits. On your first day at work you are scheduled for a two-hour conference with the company's financial counselor, Mr. Smith. During the interview, Smith takes down a complete set of information relating to your financial standing: your spouse's income and benefits, the value of family property (house, car, etc.), savings and investments, insurance coverage, the chronological, educational, and occupational status of your children, your occupational goals, the average expenditures needed to maintain your present life style, your future life-style expectations, and more. Smith then arranges to meet with you again the following week. In the meantime, Smith runs all the information through a computer.

At the second meeting, you are told that, considering your spouse's benefits from another employer, you can do without group health insurance. You can choose any one of three life insurance plans, varying in amount, options, and cost. You are also told that you should seriously consider opting for group legal insurance, perhaps even taking the package that includes divorce coverage. You also have the option of group auto insurance.

Your vacation time can be taken in any one of several forms. For instance, you can pick from these possibilities:

• Taking two weeks a year for five years, and then take a four-month sabbatical, or . . .
• Taking four weeks a year, or . . .
• Taking off one work day every other week . . .

You are also advised that you can receive part of your $23,000 total compensation in education benefits as well as in vacation and insurance benefits. Based on your financial and life-style case history, it might be wise for you to consider one of several continuing education plans available on a group basis. In addition, you can choose between several savings and pension plans, some more strongly recommended for you by the computer than others.

After considering all the options and mulling over the computer's "suggestions," you advise Smith that you have settled on a salary of $15,000 and will allocate the other $8,000 in ways you think will be best for yourself, your family, your present situation, and future objectives.

GETTING MORE PERSONAL

This scenario is hardly unique among forecasts in its potential usefulness for an individual thinking about his or her own future. Some have the ability to move us to action now, a statement for which a personal example is in order. Several years ago, when I first read the Institute for the Future's study on the future of employee benefits, I was stunned by a prediction for 1985 which said that because of the growth of employee benefits and the niceties of the big organization (like Mr. Smith and his advice-laden computer above), self-employed people would be fast vanishing from the scene. As I had left a job with a big organization shortly before that to become a self-employed writer, the idea of going on the endangered species list did not appeal to me, nor was I particularly thrilled by the notion that everybody else would soon be working for IBM, Colonel Sanders, or the government. Since then the prediction has had a real impact on me and I have taken a number of small but personally significant actions to help keep that prediction from coming true. I have, among other things, written an article on the advantages of self-employment and the need for keeping that option open to people (which was quoted in a number of places, including the Department of Health, Education and Welfare's *Work in America* report), wrote on the future of self-employment in another book, helped start a group of independent writers, which is now buying its own benefits at group rates, and I'm telling you about it now. If, as I hope, the prediction turns out to be totally wrong, it was still a "good" forecast because it forced me to act on the future.

Taking this a step further, I asked several prominent

futurists, who are usually only asked about sweeping societal developments, how they had been personally affected by futurism. The answers speak for themselves. Ed Cornish, who heads the World Future Society, says that his life has been significantly altered by projections and expert testimony on the future of energy and resources, which have led him to such direct responses as forgoing the luxury of driving to his office (he now walks) to a fundamental change in eating habits (he no longer eats meat). Cornish is deeply convinced that we are all going to have to learn to live with less, and he is preparing himself for this. Edith Weiner of the Trend Analysis Program says that she has seen several people close to the work of her program who have been forced to think about their own futures and as a result have gotten out of bad marriages, unfulfilling jobs, and old habits. Several futurists have claimed that one of the simplest levels at which people are affected is in terms of such basics as cigarette smoking, use of alcohol, overeating, and exercise. As one put it, "People who are fascinated with the next century tend to want to live to see it. I know a number of middle-aged futurists who have given up smoking for just this reason—or at least that was the final reason that got them to quit."

ALMANAC
AND
DIRECTORY

The following sections have been put together to give the reader quick, usable information on futurism. The sections range from a "Yellow Pages" meant to be used to get you into the various futures networks to a collection of model scenarios to help you learn more about how they are written. Taken together, it is hoped that these five sections will help the reader make new contacts, think new thoughts, and, in general, start thinking like a futurist.

1

THE FUTURIST'S YELLOW PAGES

The following listings and bits of information are presented to make it easier for the reader to get involved in various aspects of futurism. The listings are not all-inclusive but rather are meant to be representative of the various kinds of futuristic institutions now in existence.

New institutions are coming into being all the time and one's best source for keeping track of those are the magazines, journals, and newsletters listed under "Periodicals."

APPROPRIATE TECHNOLOGY
(SEE SOFT TECHNOLOGY.)

ASSOCIATIONS AND SOCIETIES, INTERNATIONAL

IRADES
Via Paisiello 6
00198 Roma
ITALY

An international clearinghouse for individuals and organizations involved in forecasting human trends. Publishes a newsletter and periodic directory.

World Future Society
4916 St. Elmo Avenue (Bethesda)
Washington, D.C. 20014
(301) 656-8274

See separate listing under "World Future Society" for this all-important organization.

World Future Studies Federation (WFSF)
Casella Postale 6203
Roma Prati
ITALY

WFSF's stated purpose: ". . . to promote and encourage futures studies of social relevance and to promote innovative, interdisciplinary, and critical thinking among all people." Extensive monthly newsletter.

BOOKS

In recent years hundreds of books have been published on futurism, forecasting, and specific aspects of the future. The most convenient way of getting a quick introduction to futurist literature is through the catalog of the World Future Society Book Service, which lists and summarizes the most important works in the field. Books are offered for sale to members and nonmembers alike (although members get a discount), and the catalog is free. It is also a source for future-oriented magazines, "learning kits," cassettes, and games. Write to:

The World Future Society
Book Service
4916 St. Elmo Avenue (Bethesda)
Washington, D.C. 20014

CANADIAN FUTURISTS

The most immediate way to plug into Canadian futurism is through the Canadian Association for Future Studies, which is open to anyone interested in future studies. It publishes a bulletin called *Futures Canada* (which will soon be turned into a more ambitious journal), an annual membership directory, and *The Futures Canada*

Book Review—subscriptions to all of which are covered in one's membership fee. The bulletin is a good source for news of other futures-oriented groups (The Montreal Future Society, the Canadian Center for Bioethics, the Solar Energy Society of Canada, etc.), as well as announcements of upcoming events and conferences. The three-day "Shaping the Future" conference held in June, 1977, in Kingston, Ontario, was the association's second major national conference on the future.

Regular memberships are $15 a year, students pay $7, libraries can get all publications for $9, and corporate supporting memberships begin at $50 a year. Contact:

Mrs. Margaret Wise
Membership Secretary
Canadian Association for Future Studies
c/o Faculty of Education
Althouse College
The University of Western Ontario
London, Ontario N6G 1G7
CANADA

COMPUTERS (SEE ELECTRONICS.)

CONGRESSIONAL FUTURISM

The best way of keeping up with the growing number of futures activities taking place in and around Congress is through:

The Congressional Clearinghouse on the Future
722 House Annex No. 1
Washington, D.C. 20515
(202) 225-3153

The Clearinghouse sponsors monthly seminars on the future and puts out a monthly newsletter.

Meanwhile, the center for congressional research into the future is:

The Futures Research Group
The Congressional Research Service
The Library of Congress
Washington, D.C. 20540
(202) 426-6498

Write to them for lists of the latest publications, which you can then usually obtain free from your congressperson.

CORPORATE FUTURISM

The number of corporations, trade associations, and large scientific laboratories that are involved in some aspect of futures research is large and growing. Here is a list of just some of those whose names have shown up in the literature. Space does not permit listing addresses, but these can be found in any good business directory.

AB Astra (Sweden)
Allstate Group
American Cyanamid
American Optical Corp.
Amoco Oil
Argonne National
  Laboratory
Associated Merchandising
AT&T
Atlantic Richfield
Babcock and Wilcox
Ballistic Research Labs
Bell Canada
Bendix Research Labs
Bethlehem Steel
Boeing
Boyle Engineering
Brown and Sharpe
Caterpillar Tractor
Coca-Cola
Consad Research

Dentsply International
Dow Chemical
Dow Corning
E. I. DuPont DeNemours
  and Co.
Eastman Kodak
Edison Electric
Electronics Industries
  Association
Equitable Life Assurance
  Society
Exxon Research
First National Bank of
  Minneapolis
Ford
General Electric
General Foods
General Mills
General Motors
General Research
Genesco

Grumman Aircraft
Healy Foundation
Hooker Chemical
Hydro-Quebec
Imperial Chemical
    Industries
Institute of Life Insurance
International Business
    Machines
Johnson and Johnson
Lever Brothers
Mead Corp.
Metropolitan Life
    Insurance
Mobil Oil
Monsanto
Nabisco
Olin Corp.
Owens-Corning Fiberglas
Philip Morris
Pillsbury

Polysar Ltd.
Procter and Gamble
Prudential Insurance Co.
Quaker Oats
Royal Bank of Canada
Scott Paper
Scovill
Sears
Standard Oil of Ohio
Stromberg Carlson
Sun Oil
Uni-Royal
Upjohn
Volvo
Western Electric
Westavco
Westinghouse Electric
Weyerhaeuser
Whirlpool
Xerox

COURSES

Futures courses encompassing a mind-boggling array of individual titles are being offered around the country. Samples: the Sociology of the Future (University of Alabama), Business in the 21st Century (Kent State), and the City in the World of the Future (University of Wisconsin). They are offered at the college level as well as at a growing number of high schools and adult education centers.

In trying to locate individual courses one is best advised to check with local colleges as well as in the latest editions of the directories listed under the next heading. However, the most extensive college-level programs are offered at these institutions, some of which actually offer MA's and MS's in futurism:

The Futures Planning, Forecasting and Assessment
   Program
Fairleigh Dickinson University
Madison, New Jersey 07940

Program in Business Innovation and Strategy
Florida Atlantic University
Boca Raton, Florida 33432

Program in Futures Studies
University of Hawaii
Honolulu, Hawaii 96822

Studies of the Future
University of Houston at Clear Lake City
Houston, Texas 77058

Center for Futuristic Studies
International Graduate School of Education
Parker, Colorado 80134

Program for the Study of the Future
Kean College of New Jersey
Union, New Jersey 07083

Future Studies Program
University of Massachusetts
Amherst, Massachusetts 01002

Program in Alternative Social and Educational Futures
University of Minnesota
Minneapolis, Minnesota 55409

Future Studies Program
Wittenberg University
Springfield, Ohio 45501

DIRECTORIES

Several major directories of futurists and futurists organizations have been published in recent years, but the
most useful, current, and extensive of these is *The Future:
A Guide to Information Sources*, which was compiled and
edited by the World Future Society. Among other things,
it contains capsule biographies of 450 leading individuals

in the field and lists some 600 books, reports, and periodicals. It is available from the society to nonmembers for $17.50 and to members for $15 (see address under "World Future Society" listing). The Futures Group at the Library of Congress periodically issues specialized directories (see "Congressional" listing). The American Management Association offers a directory called *Exploratory Planning Briefs* which details corporate and government futures planning groups worldwide. It is available for $15 from the AMA by writing to:

AMACOM
135 West 50th St.
New York, New York 10020

ELECTRONICS

One clear trend for the future is that computers and other electronic systems will increasingly become the province of the individual and networks of computer buffs. Two particularly convenient ways of plugging into this world are through these two magazines:

BYTE
BYTE Publications, Inc.
70 Main St.
Peterborough, New Hampshire 03458

Creative Computing
P.O. Box 789-M
Morristown, New Jersey 07960

Both magazines are lively and concerned with things like computerized gaming, do-it-yourself robotry and the like.

FILMS

Future Drugs, The Ultimate Machine, Cybernetics, Man-Made Man, 1985, Population and the American Future, Future Shock, and *View of America from the 23rd Century* are just a few of the many films, mostly short subjects, which have been made about the future. Two reference books, both published by the World Future Society, list and discuss them: *Films on the Future* by Marie Martin (1977) and *The Future: A Guide to Information Sources*. Another important reference is *Hal in the Classroom: Science Fiction Films* by Ralph J. Amelio (Pflaum, 1974).

FUTURES GROUPS

(See also separate listings for ASSOCIATIONS AND SOCIETIES, CANADIAN FUTURISTS, CONGRESSIONAL FUTURISM, CORPORATE FUTURISM, LOCAL FUTURES GROUPS OVERSEAS CONTACTS, REGIONAL FUTURES GROUPS, STATE FUTURES GROUPS THINK TANKS, and THE WORLD FUTURE SOCIETY.)

Here is a collection of the most important futures think tanks, consulting firms, forecasting groups, and centers for futuristic activity which do not appear under other listings.

Applied Futures, Inc.
22 Greenwich Plaza
Greenwich, Connecticut 06830
(203) 661-9711

A private consulting firm which also markets the CONSENSOR—a piece of futuristic hardware for getting electronic consensuses in the manner of Delphi.

Center for Futures Research
University of Southern California
University Park
Los Angeles, California 90007
(213) 746-5229

Important center for futures research, conferences, and publication. Very much concerned with new forecasting methodologies. Best known for its ambitious "Twenty-Year Forecast Project."

Center for the Study of the Future
4110 NE Alameda
Portland, Oregon 97212
(503) 282-5835

Futures research and exploration within a Christian context. Publishes, conducts seminars, and consults.

Committee for the Future
2325 Porter St.
Washington, D.C. 20008
(202) 966-8776

A Washington-based nonprofit organization conducting a variety of futures activities. Emphasis on video-related futures exploration techniques and its own conference technique called SYNCON. Its future direction was being reevaluated at the time of this writing.

Earthrise, Inc.
P.O. Box 120 Annex Station
Providence, Rhode Island 02901
(401) 274-0011

Nonprofit research group which provides a number of services. It conducts workshops on the future, Futures Lab (an undergraduate futures studies course), and the Global Futures Game. It publishes a topnotch newsletter on futures research projects around the world.

Forecasting International, Ltd.
1001 North Highland St.
Arlington, Virginia 22201
(703) 527-1311

Leading private research group.

Foundation for the Future
Inn Street Mall and Market Square
Box 2001
Newburyport, Massachusetts 01950
(617) 462-8900

Educational group which publishes the newsletter *Future Report*. Has an extensive collection of futures-related material and conducts futures events (fairs, expos, conferences).

Future Options Room
1223 Connecticut Avenue NW
Washington, D.C. 20036
(202) 393-1970

A very active new group which, among other things, produces reports, films, slide shows, courses, and displays on future-related topics.

FUTUREMICS, Inc.
2850 Connecticut Avenue NW
Washington, D.C. 20008
(202) 667-5620

Private research and educational group involved in a number of specific activities ranging from the development of futures-related courses and educational program to the production of *Futures-Abstracts,* a card-system which summarizes new developments in the field. It also publishes the highly informative newsletter *Footnotes to the Future.*

Futures Conditional
Northwest Regional Foundation
P.O. Box 5296
Spokane, Washington 99205
(509) 455-9255

A magazine and a concept designed to help people think about their options for the future. Anyone seriously interested in the future should write for more information.

The Future Group, Inc.
124 Hebron Avenue
Glastonbury, Connecticut 06033
(203) 633-6743

Leading private futures research and consulting firm discussed in detail in Chapter 3.

The Futures Invention Project
Syracuse Research Corp.
Merrill Lane
Syracuse, New York 13210
(315) 425-5100

A group primarily concerned with running workshops to help individuals and groups invent their own futures. Has worked with colleges, religious groups, and communities.

Futures Research Institute
Portland State University
P.O. Box 751
Portland, Oregon 97207
(503) 229-4960

Conducts research and conferences.

The Hudson Institute
Quaker Ridge Road
Croton-on-Hudson, New York 10520
(914) 762-0700

Leading think tank concerned with the future. Dominated by Herman Kahn.

Information Futures
2217 College Station
Pullman, Washington 99163
(509) 332-5762

Consulting group which develops conferences, seminars, workshops, and reports in response to specific needs.

Institute for the Future
2725 Sand Hill Road
Menlo Park, California 92405
(415) 854-6322

Nonprofit institute which is a key force in futurism. Offers an extensive list of research reports.

Interrobang Ideas
c/o Gus Jaccaci
Common Street
Groton, Massachusetts 01450

An ad hoc creative group which stages futurist events—workshops, futuristic town meetings, and future games.

Predicasts, Inc.
200 University Circle Research Center
11001 Cedar Avenue
Cleveland, Ohio 44106
(216) 795-3000

Large business information and forecasting group.

Princeton Center for Alternative Futures, Inc.
60 Hodge Road
Princeton, New Jersey 08540
(609) 921-2280

Private research and education group.

The RAND Corporation
1700 Main Street
Santa Monica, California 90406
(213) 393-0411

Major multifaceted think tank which did much of the pioneering work in the field of technological forecasting. Much of its current work is future-oriented.

Resources for the Future, Inc.
1755 Massachusetts Avenue NW
Washington, D.C. 20036
(202) 462-4400

Key research unit concerned with the future of natural resources. Extensive publications program.

Stanford Research Institute
Center for the Study of Social Policy
333 Ravenswood Avenue
Menlo Park, California 94025
(415) 326-6200

Major futures research group whose work is discussed in Chapter 5.

Trend Analysis Program
Institute of Life Insurance
277 Park Avenue
New York, New York 10017
(212) 922-3041

Innovative research unit profiled in Chapter 4.

Charles W. Williams, Inc.
801 North Pitt St.
Alexandria, Virginia 22314
(703) 548-2501

Private futures research group.

Worldwatch Institute
1776 Massachusetts Avenue NW
Washington, D.C. 20036
(202) 452-1999

New think tank concerned with identifying and solving emerging world problems.

GAMES

There has been tremendous growth in futuristic games in recent years. Herewith some sources and their products.

John D. W. Andrews
810 Crest Road
Del Mar, California 92014

Resource Dynamics: 2000 AD.

Ken Davis
Dept. of English
University of Kentucky
Lexington, Kentucky 40506

The Utopia Game

Earth Metabolic Design
Box 2016 Yale Station
New Haven, Connecticut 06520

Buckminster Fuller's World Game . . . runs World Game Conferences.

Jerry Debenham
Dept. of Educational Administration
University of Utah
Milton Bennion Hall
Salt Lake City, Utah 84112

SAFE (Simulated Alternative Futures in Education)

Earthrise, Inc.
P.O. Box 120 Annex Station
Providence, Rhode Island 02901

Global Futures Game and workshops associated with it.

Interact
Box 262
Lakeside, California 92040

Cope, Interact

League of Women Voters
1730 M St. NW
Washington, D.C. 20036

Exploring American Futures, Play the Futures Game

Metagaming Concepts
Box 15346
Austin, Texas 78761

Source for more than a score of science fiction and fantasy games (*Stellar Conquest, Star Lord*, etc.) and the publisher of *The Space Gamer*, a bimonthly magazine.

New Games Foundation
P.O. Box 7901
San Francisco, California 94120

Outdoor games for the aquarian age: *Boffers, Earthball, Fraha*, etc.

SIMILE II
218 Twelfth St.
P.O. Box 910
Del Mar, California 92014

Metropolitics, SITTE, Starpower, Bafa Bafa, etc.

Simulation and Gaming Association
4833 Greentree Rd.
Lebanon, Ohio 45036

*Future Decisions: The IQ Game, Design Your Own Game,
Kama,* etc.

TSR Hobbies, Inc.
P.O. Box 756
Lake Geneva, Wisconsin 53147

Starprobe, Metamorphosis Alpha, and other science fiction and fantasy games.

World Future Society
4916 St. Elmo Avenue (Bethesda)
Washington, D.C. 20014

Distributes *Futuribles, New Town, Future Shock,* and other games.

LOCAL FUTURES GROUPS

Some, but by no means all.

Atlanta 2000, Inc.
c/o Robert Hanie
Executive Director
1320 Healey Bldg.
Atlanta, Georgia 30303
(404) 577-5654

Goals for Greater Akron
Barbara Hiney
Executive Director
One Cascade Plaza,
8th floor
Akron, Ohio 44308
(216) 375-2176

Austin Tomorrow
Tracy Watson
Advanced Planning
Supervisor
City of Austin Planning
Dept.
P.O. Box 1088
Austin, Texas 78767
(512) 477-6511

Central Virginia Tomorrow
Herbert R. Moore
412 Madison St.
Lynchburg, Virginia 24501
(804) 847-9059

Dimensions for Charlotte-
Mecklenburg
Dr. James Cox
Director
Institute for Urban
Studies and Community
Service
University of North
Carolina
Charlotte, North Carolina
28223
(704) 597-2307

Goals for Dallas
Dr. Bryghte Godbold
Director
Suite 825
1 Main Place
Dallas, Texas 75250
(214) 741-1738

Independence Neighbor-
hood Councils
P.O. Box 407
Independence, Missouri
64051
(816) 833-4225

Goals for Raleigh/Wake
Betty Doak
Executive Director
Box 17022
Raleigh, North Carolina
27609
(919) 787-4218

Seattle 2000
Douglass Raff
4300 Seattle
1st National Bank Bldg.
Seattle, Washington 98154
(206) 624-3600

OVERSEAS CONTACTS

Club of Rome
c/o Mr. Aurelio Peccei
Via Giorgione 163
00147 Rome
ITALY

Institute for Future
Technology
Science Museum 2–1
Kitanomaru-Koen
Chiyoda-ku
Tokyo 102
JAPAN

Institute for Future Studies
Vester Farimågsgade 3
DK-1606 Copenhagen V
DENMARK

International Association
Futuribles-France
(A.I.F.)
10 Rue Cernuschi
F. 75017 Paris
FRANCE

International Creative
  Center
20, ch. Colladon, 1211
Geneva 28
SWITZERLAND

International Institute for
  Applied Systems Analysis
  (IIASA)
Schloss Platz 1
Laxenburg, A-2361
AUSTRIA

Mankind 2000
1 Rue aux Laines
1000 Brussels
BELGIUM

Plan Europe 2000
European Cultural
  Foundation
5 Jan Van Goyenkade
Amsterdam 1007
NETHERLANDS

Secretariat for Future
  Studies
P.O. Box S-103 10
Stockholm
SWEDEN

Society for Long-Range
  Planning
8th floor
Terminal House
Grosvenor Gardens
London SW1W OAR
ENGLAND

The Swedish Association of
  Future Studies
Royal Swedish Academy of
  Engineering Sciences
  (IVA)
Box 5073
102 42 Stockholm 5
SWEDEN

USSR Academy of Sciences
Section on Social
  Forecasting
Institute of Social Research
Novo-Cheremushki 46
Moscow 117418
USSR

World Future Society
London Group
45, Bromley Common
Bromley, Kent
ENGLAND

PEACEFUL FUTURES

The Canadian Peace Research Institute
119 Thomas St.
Oakville, Ontario L6J 3A7
(416) 845-9370

Long-established institution working to establish ground rules for a new branch of science—peace research. It has an active publication and research program and issues a periodic *News Report*.

Center for Peace Studies
University of Akron
Akron, Ohio 44304
(216) 375-7008

Offers an undergraduate program in Peace Studies, conducts research, and publishes *The International Peace Studies Newsletter*.

Center for Peaceful Change
Kent State University
Kent State, Ohio 44242
(216) 672-3143

Offers program of study and research geared to peaceful change in human systems.

Consortium on Peace Research, Education and Development (COPRED)
c/o Norman V. Walbek
Executive Director
Gustavus Adolphus College
St. Peter, Minnesota 56082
(507) 931-4300

National organization which assists and supports peace education and research. More than 100 institutions are now associated with COPRED.

Emergency Committee for World Government
Frederick Hendriklaan 26
The Hague, Netherlands

International group pushing for democratic world government.

Institute for World Order, Inc.
1140 Avenue of the Americas
New York, New York 10036
(212) 575-0055

Research group whose projects include the World Order Models Project and the follow-on Lodi Project—efforts aimed at constructing models of the world in the year 2000 in which the four values of peace, social justice, economic well-being, and ecological balance are realized.

International Peace Research Institute
P.O. Box 5052
Oslo 3
NORWAY

A key center for peace thinking and research. Publishes two influential journals: *The Journal of Peace Research* and *The Bulletin of Peace Proposals* (both in English).

National Peace Academy Campaign
1629 K St. NW
Suite 400
Washington, D.C. 20006
(202) 466-2442

Group working to create the equivalent of a West Point for teaching conflict resolution and peace-keeping.

Peace Studies Institute and Program in Conflict
    Resolution
Manchester College
North Manchester, Indiana 46962

Courses, publications, consultant services, and conference and workshop planning.

Planetary Citizens
777 United Nations Plaza
New York, New York 10017

Moving toward "an awareness of the world as one single environment and of mankind as one human family." Maintains a registry of those who have declared their new allegiance to mankind as a whole by endorsing its *Manifesto and Pledge of Planetary Citizenship* and issues its own "Planetary Passport."

Promoting Enduring Peace, Inc.
P.O. Box 103
Woodmont, Connecticut 06460
(203) 878-4769

Religious and educational organization which conducts international peace seminars, distributes articles having to do with world peace, and gives the annual Gandhi Peace Award.

Stockholm International Peace Research Institute
　(SIPRI)
Sveavagen 166
S-113 46 Stockholm
SWEDEN

Leading international, independent peace research institute which is best known for its yearbook on arms and arms control.

World Constitution and Parliament Association
1480 Hoyt St.
Suite 31
Lakewood, Colorado 80215
(303) 233-3548

Group devoted to the goals in its name.

War Control Planners, Inc.
Box 19127
Washington, D.C. 20036
(202) 785-0708

Unit promoting world safety and de-escalation through technology. Publishes *Checkpoint,* a newsletter "for people concerned with future civilized global systems."

World Peace News
777 UN Plaza—11th floor
New York, New York 10017

Lively, iconoclastic tabloid

PERIODICALS

(Magazines and journals designated [m] and newsletters [nl]. The address of the World Future Society and information on subscribing to its various periodicals appear under the heading "World Future Society.")

Business Tomorrow (nl)
   World Future Society
Careers Tomorrow (nl)
   World Future Society
Communications Tomorrow (nl)
   World Future Society
Earthrise Newsletter (nl)
   Earthrise, Inc.
   P.O. Box 120 Annex Station
   Providence, Rhode Island 02901
Ekistics (m)
   Athens Center of Ekistics
   24 Strat. Syndesmou St.
   P.O. Box 471
   Athens 135, Attica
   GREECE
Food Tomorrow (nl)
   World Future Society
Footnotes to the Future (nl)
   Futuremics, Inc.
   2850 Connecticut Avenue NW
   Washington, D.C. 20008
Future-Abstracts
   Futuremics, Inc.
   (same address as above)
Future Report (nl)
   Foundation for the Future
   Inn Street Mall and Market Square
   Box 2001
   Newburyport, Massachusetts 01950

Futures (m)
  IPC Science and Technology Press Ltd.
  IPC House
  32 High Street
  Guildford Surrey, England GU1 3EW
Futures Conditional (m)
  Northwest Regional Foundation
  P.O. Box 5296
  Spokane, Washington 99205
The Futures Information Newsletter (nl)
  Futures Information Network
  c/o Manfred Kochen
  Mental Health Research Institute
  University of Michigan
  Ann Arbor, Michigan 48109
The Futurist (m)
  World Future Society
Government Tomorrow (nl)
  World Future Society
Habitats Tomorrow (nl)
  World Future Society
Hastings Center Report (m)
  Institute of Society, Ethics and the Life Sciences
  360 Broadway
  Hastings-on-Hudson, New York 10706
Health Tomorrow (nl)
  World Future Society
Human Values Tomorrow (nl)
  World Future Society
Important for the Future (m)
  United Nations Institute for Training and Research
  801 United Nations Plaza
  New York, New York 10017
International Affairs Tomorrow (nl)
  World Future Society
J-M Future (m)
  Johns-Manville Corp.
  Greenwood Plaza
  Denver, Colorado 80217

Life-Styles Tomorrow (nl)
   World Future Society
Long-Range Planning (m)
   Pergamon Press Ltd.
   Headington Hill Hall
   Oxford
   ENGLAND
Practicing Planner (m)
   American Institute of Planners
   1776 Massachusetts Avenue NW
   Washington, D.C. 20036
Resources (nl)
   Resources for the Future
   1755 Massachusetts Avenue NW
   Washington, D.C. 20036
Resources Tomorrow (nl)
   World Future Society
Social Innovation (m)
   Thor, Inc.
   1506 19th St. NW
   Washington, D.C. 20036
Technological Forecasting and Social Change (m)
   American Elsevier Publishing Co., Inc.
   52 Vanderbilt Avenue
   New York, New York 10017
Technology Forecasts and Technology Surveys (nl)
   Suite 208
   208 S. Beverly Drive
   Beverly Hills, California 90212
Technology Tomorrow (nl)
   World Future Society
Working Papers for a New Society (m)
   The Center for the Study of Public Policy, Inc.
   123 Mount Auburn St.
   Cambridge, Massachusetts 02138
World Future Society Bulletin (m)
   World Future Society

REGIONAL FUTURES GROUPS

Great Lakes Tomorrow, Inc.
Richard Robbins
c/o Lake Michigan Federation
53 West Jackson Blvd.
Chicago, Illinois 60604
(312) 427-5121

Northwest Regional Foundation
Robert L. Stilger
Executive Director
P.O. Box 5296
Spokane, Washington 99205
(509) 455-9255

Commission on the Future of the South
E. Evan Brunson
Southern Growth Policies Board
P.O. Box 12293
Research Triangle Park, North Carolina 27709
(919) 549-8169

SOFT TECHNOLOGY

Also known as alternative, appropriate, and intermediate technology. Here are some key names and addresses and journals to help get you into this network.

Center for Studies in Food Self-Sufficiency
Vermont Institute of Community Involvement
90 Main St.
Burlington, Vermont 05401
Decentralized agriculture.

The Co-Evolution Quarterly
P.O. Box 428
Sausalito, California 94965

The Whole Earth Catalog in a new format. Just as fascinating as the original.

Institute for Local Self-Reliance
1717 18th St. NW
Washington, D.C. 20009
(202) 232-4108

Bidding to be the prime think tank for soft technology. Concerns: urban energy sources, urban food production, community governance, community economics, information access, waste utilization.

The New Alchemy Institute
P.O. Box 432
Woods Hole, Massachusetts 02543

Major center for experimentation.

Rain
Journal of Appropriate Technology
2270 NW Irving
Portland, Oregon 97210
(503) 227-5110

A lively magazine for keeping in touch with the rest of the movement. Each issue is loaded with information on such things as energy saving, food, shelter, recycling, "good things," etc.

TRANET (transnational network for appropriate/alternative technologies)
c/o W. N. Ellis
7410 Vernon Square Drive
Alexandria, Virginia 22306

Clearinghouse for soft technology groups worldwide.

SPACE (INNER)

Aquarian Research Foundation
5620 Morton St.
Philadelphia, Pennsylvania 19144
(215) 849-3237

Research and information on altered states of consciousness, healing, spiritual phenomena, and the like.

ESP Laboratory
7559 Santa Monica Blvd.
Los Angeles, California 90046
(213) 876-9984

Offers a variety of ESP-related services including a newsletter and ESP development classes.

The Foundation for Mind Research
P.O. Box 600
Pomona, New York 10970
(914) 354-4965

Research group exploring inner potentials. The work of this group is detailed in an article in the February 22, 1975, issue of *Saturday Review* entitled "Putting the First Man on Earth."

Mankind Research Unlimited, Inc.
Washington, D.C. 20005
(201) 882-4000

Multifaceted group doing research and developing hardware for various nonconventional specific areas. MRU's major concerns include Kirlian photography, acupuncture, bioenergetics, ESP phenomena, biofeedback, and meditation.

Mind Science Foundation
7335 East 6th Avenue
Scottsdale, Arizona 85251
(602) 946-7730

Developing methods and techniques for better physical, mental, and spiritual health.

Parapsychology Foundation, Inc.
29 West 57th St.
New York, New York 10019
(212) 751-5940

Group whose efforts are directed toward encouraging research and experimentation in parapsychology and the paranormal. It has a research library.

SPACE (OUTER)

Here are some groups that operate outside the normal channels (NASA, the Air Force, the large aerospace corporations, etc.), bidding to have an influence on the future of space.

Earth/Space, Inc.
4151 Middlefield

Palo Alto, California 94303
(415) 494-8339

Stresses the role of free enterprise and profits in space. Produces *Earth/Space News*.

FASST (Forum for the Advancement of Students in Science and Technology, Inc.)
1785 Massachusetts Avenue NW
Washington, D.C. 20036
(202) 483-2900

Broad-based student science and technical group with a keen interest in space. It works to get students involved in space programs and as this was written was campaigning to get students on the space shuttle.

The Foundation Institute
Suite 704
810 Thornton St. SE
Minneapolis, Minnesota 55414
(612) 332-6621
Advocates private enterprise in space.

L-5 Society
1620 North Park Avenue
Tucson, Arizona 85719

Formed to tell of the benefits and potentials of space colonization, space industrialization, and satellite solar power. Its principle vehicle is the *L-5 News*. Says James Kempf, a spokesman for the society, "Our stated goal is to eventually disband at a space colony located at L-5."

Public Interest Satellite Association (PISA)
55 West 44th St.
New York, New York 10036
(212) 730-5172

Advocates greater public-interest use of satellite communications technology. Much concerned with getting non-profit groups into the act.

United for Our Expanded Space Program
Post Office Box 7807
San Diego, California 92107

Toward a bigger and better space effort.

STATE FUTURES GROUPS

California Tomorrow
Monadnock Bldg.
681 Market St.
San Francisco, California
   94105
(415) 391-7544

Delaware Tomorrow
   Commission
State Planning Office
Thomas Collins Bldg.
Dover, Delaware 19901
(302) 678-4271

Hawaii Commission on the
   Year 2000
c/o Gerald Sumida
Carlsmith, Carlsmith, Wich-
   man and Case
Suite 2200
Pacific Trade Center
Honolulu, Hawaii 96813
(808) 524-5112

Idaho's Tomorrow
Division of Budget, Policy,
   Planning and
   Coordination
State House
Boise, Idaho 83720
(208) 384-3900

Iowa 2000
c/o Institute of Public
   Affairs
University of Iowa
Iowa City, Iowa 52242
(319) 353-7228

Commission on Maine's
   Future
184 State Street
Augusta, Maine 04333
(207) 289-3261

Massachusetts Tomorrow
61 Chestnut St.
West Newton, Massachusetts
   02165
(617) 235-5320

Commission on Minnesota's
   Future
101 Capitol Square Bldg.
St. Paul, Minnesota 55101
(612) 296-3852

Vermont Tomorrow
c/o Dave Goldberg
5 State St.
Montpelier, Vermont 05602
(802) 223-6067

Alternatives for Washington
c/o Dr. Edward Lindaman
President
Whitworth College
Home Estates
Spokane, Washington
   99218
(509) 489-3550

THINK TANKS

By their very nature think tanks are future-oriented, so these names and addresses are given in addition to those entirely futuristic groups listed under FUTURES GROUPS.

The Academy for Contemporary Problems
1501 Neil Avenue
Columbus, Ohio 43201
(614) 421-7700

Analytic Services, Inc. (ANSER)
5613 Leesburg Pike
Falls Church, Virginia 22041
(703) 820-2830

Arthur D. Little, Inc.
25 Acorn Park
Cambridge, Massachusetts 02140
(617) 864-5770

Battelle Memorial Institute
505 King Avenue
Columbus, Ohio 43201
(614) 424-6424

The Brookings Institution
1775 Massachusetts Avenue NW
Washington, D.C. 20036
(202) 797-6000

CALSPAN Corp.
P.O. Box 235
Buffalo, New York 14221
(716) 632-7500

Center for Policy Research
475 Riverside Avenue
New York, New York 10027
(212) 870-2180

Center for the Study of Democratic Institutions
P.O. Box 4068
Santa Barbara, California 93103
(805) 969-3281

Denver Research Institute
University Park
Denver, Colorado 80210
(303) 753-2271

Franklin Institute
Benjamin Franklin Parkway at 20th St.
Philadelphia, Pennsylvania 19103
(215) 448-1000

General Research Corp.
5383 Hollister Avenue
Santa Barbara, California 93105

The Hastings Institute of Society, Ethics and the Life Sciences
360 Broadway
Hastings-on-Hudson, New York 10706
(914) 478-0500

IIT (Illinois Institute of
Technology) Research
Institute
10 West 35th St.
Chicago, Illinois 60616
(312) 567-4000

Institute for Advanced
Study
Alden Lane
Princeton, New Jersey
08540
(609) 924-4400

Institute for Defense
Analyses
400 Army-Navy Drive
Arlington, Virginia 22202
(703) 558-1000

Institute for Policy Studies
1901-1909 Q Street NW
Washington, D.C. 20009
(202) 234-9382

Lincoln Laboratory
244 Wood Street
Lexington, Massachusetts
02173
(617) 862-5500

Mathematica, Inc.
Princeton Station Office
Park
P.O. Box 2392
Princeton, New Jersey
08540
(609) 799-2600

Midwest Research Institute
425 Volker Blvd.
Kansas City, Missouri
64110
(816) 561-0202

The MITRE Corp.
P.O. Box 208
Bedford, Massachusetts
01730
(617) 271-2000

National Planning Asso-
ciation
1606 New Hampshire Ave-
nue NW
Washington, D.C. 20009
(202) 265-7685

Operations Research, Inc.
1400 Spring Street
Silver Spring, Maryland
20910
(301) 588-6180

Planning Research Corp.
1100 Glendon Avenue
Los Angeles, California
90024
(213) 479-7725

R&D Associates
4640 Admiralty Way
Marina del Rey, California
90291
(213) 822-1715

Southwest Research Insti-
tute
8500 Culebra Road
San Antonio, Texas 78228
(512) 684-5111

Stanford Research Institute
333 Ravenwood Avenue
Menlo Park, California
  94025
(415) 326-6200

System Development Corp.
2500 Colorado Avenue
Santa Monica, California
  90406
(213) 829-7511

TEMPO (Technical, Environmental and Management Planning Operation)
816 State St.
P.O. Drawer QQ
Santa Barbara, California
  93102
(805) 965-0551

The Urban Institute
2100 M St. NW
Washington, D.C. 20037
(202) 223-1950

Western Behavioral Sciences Institute
1150 Silverado Drive
La Jolla, California 92037
(714) 459-3811

UFOLOGISTS

Some futurists would dispute the appearance of these groups in such a directory, but if they are right they are indeed futurists.

Aerial Phenomena Research Organization, Inc. (APRO)
3910 E. Kleindale Road
Tucson, Arizona 85712
(602) 793-1825

Center for UFO Studies
924 Chicago Avenue
Evanston, Illinois 60202

National Investigations Committee on Aerial Phenomena (NICAP)
Suite 23
3535 University Blvd. West
Kensington, Maryland 20795
(301) 949-1267

THE WORLD FUTURE SOCIETY

Membership group which is more than 20,000 strong that has been the major force in the popularization of futurism in the United States and to some extent the rest of the world. Its most famous product is the bimonthly slick magazine *The Futurist* (which is sent as part of the annual dues of $15), but it also:

- Maintains a mail-order book service and "Bookstore of the Future" at its Bethesda, Maryland, headquarters.
- Provides a network of chapters in the United States and overseas which enables futurists to meet on a local level.
- Publishes a number of specialized periodicals besides *The Futurist*, including its specialized newsletters in a number of specific fields (*Careers Tomorrow, Habitats Tomorrow*, etc.).
- Periodically convenes large general assemblies on the future, which brings futurists together from all over the world.
- Runs an employment service for those looking for or trying to fill future-oriented jobs.

Anyone with a serious interest in the future should consider joining the society. Write to:

World Future Society
4916 St. Elmo Avenue (Bethesda)
Washington, D.C. 20014

2

CHARTING THE YET-TO-COME

Lists, Charts, and Tables to Help Get Us from Here to There

Like compulsive shoppers, those who dwell in the future tense tend to love to make concise lists. The reasons for this are not entirely clear, but it is a way to save time and space while quickly giving us a lot to chew on, which in itself can be seen as a break from the verbose past. We have already sampled some of these (such as the one at the end of Chapter 2), but there are a number of others which beg wider circulation as vehicles for helping us to confront the future.

Here is a small selection which the author has collected for the purpose of sparking as much extra future thinking as possible in the least number of pages. Individually they serve as devices for thinking about one aspect of the future; collectively they are meant to serve as a "crammer" for futurist thinking (not unlike those laminated notebook sheets which reduce Sociology 1–2, or whatever, to two crammed sides of economical copy set in tiny type).

1. THE FOUR FUTURE VIEWS

(There have been a number of attempts to come up with a set of categories into which all futurists can be sorted. One that seems to work better than most is this set created by Robert Theobald.)

a. *Positive extrapolators*, who project "the best" of today into tomorrow.

b. *Negative extrapolators*, who expect the worst as today's troubles and problems become our future ruination.

c. *Synergists*, who see opportunities and dangers, pluses and minuses, etc., ahead.

d. *Jeremiahs*, who, like Old Testament prophets, see little hope ahead unless we "mend our ways."

2. CHARACTERISTICS OF A FUTURIST

(An abbreviated version of a summary created by the World Future Society in its study "An Introduction to the Study of the Future" for the National Science Foundation.)

a. *Openness to Experience* . . . appear to be remarkably open to all types of ideas; in fact, they seem to be constantly searching for new information about the world and are never so happy as when they have found a genuinely exciting idea . . .

b. *Global Perspective* . . . They all seem to think in global rather than national terms . . .

c. *Long-Term Time-Perspective* . . .

d. *Ecological Orientation* . . .

e. *Broad Concern for Humanity* . . .

f. *Rationality*. Though open to experience, futurists quickly reject notions that lack an adequate scientific or rational basis . . .

g. *Pragmatism*. As a group, the futurists seem to be primarily interested in what will "work" . . . The test of effectiveness is not any ideology of left or right—but good data and methods, genuine concern about people, and realistic assessments . . .

h. *Reality of Choice* . . . deeply conscious of the freedom of individuals to make decisions that will have tremendous consequences for good or ill . . .

i. *Interest in Values* . . . The criteria by which one decides what to choose.

j. *Optimism* . . . generally seem to believe that mankind will survive and perhaps prosper in the years ahead . . .

k. *Sense of Purpose* . . . They seem to feel that what they are doing is important and will help to create a better world.

3. HOW THE YEAR 2000 WILL DIFFER FROM THE WORLD OF TODAY IF PRESENT TRENDS CONTINUE

(Another World Future Society list from their National Science Foundation study. Condensed.)

a. *More Unified.* Improved communications and transportation will increasingly bind people into an integrated world community.

b. *More Standardized.* The metric system will be universally accepted. English will likely be the accepted lingua franca of mankind . . . A world currency may be in use . . . etc.

c. *More Affluent.* The average person in the Western world will have a relatively higher standard of living . . .

d. *More Leisured.* People will spend less time at their jobs.

e. *Less Integrated by Family and Kinship.* People will change mates more frequently. The family will have deteriorated still further and people will have increased emotional problems . . .

f. *Less Oriented Toward Industry in the Developed Countries and Less Toward Agriculture in the Developing Countries* . . .

g. *Longer Living.* Life expectancy will have reached new highs in the developing countries . . .

h. *More Mobile.* People will move about with increased frequency—both for business and pleasure.

i. *Less Religous.* Belief in the spiritual realm will have declined. More people will be unchurched.

j. *Better Educated* . . .

4. A "FROM/TO" LIST ON THE FUTURE OF EDUCATION

(A common format used by futurists to express a shift in one set of values to another is the "from/to" list. The example that follows charts major shifts that its author sees beginning to take place in education. It is by Robert E. Weber, Director of the Project on Human Potential and the Year 2000, who used it to summarize a much broader investigation.)

From old emphasis on	To new emphasis on
closed systems	open systems
traditionally credentialed personnel	noncredentialed personnel and those having multiple credentials
inefficient information transfer	educational technology
authoritarianism	humanism
arbitrary curriculums	life itself and student interests
input measurement	output measurement
white working and middle-class orientation	cultural pluralism
mass education	individual education
the needs of the economy	the needs of the individual and society
lock step	primacy of individual differences
rote learning	discovery
K-12 (kindergarten through 12th grade)	early childhood development and adult continuing education
"cells and bells" learning	home learning, independent study, learning when you feel like it
poor instructional art	scientific basis of instruction
passive learners	active learners, student-initiated learning
prohibition of use of peer resources	maximum utilization of peer resources, especially cross-peer teaching

From old emphasis on	*To new emphasis on*
external rewards	internal rewards
"student as nigger"	highly valued individual
purely cognitive	balance between cognitive, affective, and conative
conforming behavior	divergent behavior
discipline	academic excellence
fragmentation of knowledge	unity and synthesis of knowledge
grades	continuous progress
arbitrary grouping	grouping based on educational mission
competition	cooperation
memorization/regurgitation	learning to learn
suspicion	trust
punitiveness	encouragement
rewards for only academic learning	value of extra-academic learning
competency based on attendance/course completion	student-initiated "challenge" exams
school/state requirements	self-actualization
limiting of potential	expanded consciousness
teacher autonomy	learner autonomy
student dependency on teacher stimulus	chemical/electrical enhancement of learning receptivity
limited curriculum	vastly expanded curriculum
book learning	meditation, sentics, biofeedback
classroom learning	monastic learning, environmental learning

5. HANDY GUIDE TO PUBLIC POLICY PROPOSERS AND THEIR PROPOSALS

(Saving the best for last, this chart has become a much-Xeroxed satirical classic used to separate one future view from another. It was written by Michael Marien, now co-director of the Futures Information Network, and first appeared in the *Public Administration Review*, Vol. XXX, No. 2, March/April, 1970.)

General Guidelines for Post-Industrial Citizenship: (1) Pick up any position or combination thereof; (2) Don't look at other policy proposers—you are right.

Ideological Positions	View of Present and Future	Proposals for Future
1. Horrified Humanist	A slim chance of surviving our chaos and obsolescence	Sweeping reforms, world government, national planning
2. Languishing Liberal	Troubled times	More money and programs, racial integration
3. Middling Moderate	No thoughts: cross-pressured	Various platitudes to avoid offending other policy proposers
4. Counteracting Conservative	Crime, centralization, and crumbling civilization	Law, order, soap, haircuts, Truth and Morality
5. Rabid Rightist	It's getting REDDER all the time	Wave flags and stockpile arms (public and private)
6. Primitive Populist	Domination by pointy-headed pseudo-intellectuals	Throw briefcases in Potomac, restore common sense
7. Passionate Pacifist	A garrison state	A peaceable kingdom
8. Radical Romantic	A cancered civilization	Small experimental communities
9. Rumbling Revolutionary	A repressive, racist, imperialist, capitalist establishment	Confront and destroy the System (other details worked out later)
10. Apocalyptic Apostle	Armageddon coming to a sinful world	Be saved

Role-related Positions

1. Urgent Urbanist	Decline and fall of cities	More funds and programs side-stepping states
2. Emphatic Ecologist	Decline and fall of everything else	Control contaminators and restore nature
3. Boiling Blackman	Here a pig, there a pig, everywhere a pig pig	Black everything
4. Status-Seeking Sibling Sender	Crisis in our schools and colleges	More funds and programs, tax deductions
5. Multi-Mega-muscled Militarist	Growing Chinese and/or Russian capabilities	More National Security regardless of national security
6. Technocrat-on-the-Take	No thoughts: not within scope of specialty	Well-funded studies and use of arcane models
7. Sincerely Sorry Scientist	Profligate technology	Think of alternative futures and their consequences
8. Bullied Budget-Binder	Uptight	Making this year's budget and getting more for next year
9. Tortured Taxpayer	Growing gaps between income, aspirations, and expenditures	Cut, cut, cut, cut, cut, cut
10. Stultified Student	Entrapment in *their* world	Inner and interpersonal exploration, and other relevant learning
11. Contracting Conglomerator	Cybernation, diversification, and internationalization	Withering of the state

Role-related Positions

12. Hi-throttle Highway-man	Paving the nation	Re-paving the nation
13. Frustrated Feminist	Futility, frivolity, and frigidaires	Fun-filled fulfill-ment
14. Star-Struck Spaceman	Up, up, and away	Science must not be impeded
15. Bonded Bureaucrat	Six years to retirement	Longer coffee breaks

3

BONUS SCENARIOS
Further Examples of the
State of the Art

While a number of future scenarios have already appeared
within the context of the book, the author has encountered
hundreds of others. Among them have been some which
are exciting, well-written, provocative and, above all, useful devices for thinking about the future. Because of this
and the fact that most have had extremely limited distribution, it was felt that a small bonus collection of them
was in order.*

1. ONE OF THE MANY ALTERNATIVE LIFE CYCLES THE FUTURE MIGHT OFFER

THE LIFE OF JOHN SMITH: 1985–2070

Birthplace: Chicago   *Status of Mother:* Single, Age 27

Age 1 year–   Attended elementary school.
8 years:

Age 8:   Traveled with a class of fifteen students. Visited
a number of countries around the world. Learned
several languages and cultures.

Age 10:   Returned to the United States and resumed formal studies.

* All are used with the permission of the institutions which created them.

Age 15: Entered a rotating work-study program, electing to serve as an apprentice in three fields: architecture, social research, and communications science.

Age 18: Went back to formal studies in the liberal arts. Also took advanced courses in architecture.

Age 19: Spent three years abroad, studying comparative architecture.

Age 22: Returned to the United States and was employed as a draftsman. Lived for two years in an urban commune with nine other young professionals.

Age 24: Moved into an apartment with three friends—two female and one male. They were all "married" to each other, and all income and properties were pooled.

Age 27: Divorced himself from his living arrangements and married a woman who was also divorced. She had one child, aged 6. Took and passed his architectural exams.

Age 35: He and his wife took two-year leaves from their jobs, took their 14-year-old son and went to live on Nantucket. There, the three of them jointly developed their interests in the arts: painting, sketching, and sculpting.

Age 38: Divorced his wife and lived by himself.

Age 50: Set up house with two career women in their mid-forties. The relationship was economic and sexual, but not exclusive . . . he dated other women and they dated other men.

Age 60: Left his job and residence, and went to teach communications science to students in a developing country.

Age 65: Returned to the United States and resumed work part-time. Also went back to school part-time to update his formal education.

Age 67: Remarried. His new wife had two children, both grown with children of their own.

Age 72: Took a two-year leave and he, his wife, and one of their grandchildren traveled around the world. The 16-year-old grandchild remained with a family in London. He and his wife returned home.

Age 74: Resumed work and school. Became interested in photography. Developed it as a full-time hobby and part-time income.

Age 80: Took on a teaching position at a nearby university. His students ranged in age from 12 to 87. His topic was comparative architecture.

Age 85: Died of sudden lung failure.

This scenario was created by the Trend Analysis Program to show how the individual in the future will break out of the traditional four-part life cycle of preschool, school, work, and retirement. Smith's bio has become much Xeroxed from the original *TAP Report* (February, 1974) in which it appeared by those looking for a starting point for discussing the future of the individual. Often Smith's already complex life is embellished to see what effect such factors as cloning and personality modification have on it. A futures study group centered within the New Jersey Department of Education took it to the level John/Jane Smith as reported by one of its members: "At another of our futures studies seminars the embryologist Robert Francouer suggested that children born today might live, on the average, 105 to 115 years and that the technology was upon us that would enable us to live half of that life as a member of one sex and the other as a member of the other sex. He then went on to construct a scenario of stupefying moral and legal complication.

2. THE SALE OF LIFE INSURANCE IN THE YEAR 1990

A computer terminal serves as the center for entertainment and communications in almost every home. Through this medium, the home is linked to a variety of information centers, which can be reached by use of a push-button code.

Each year an individual can request a personal financial status review, accompanied by a print-out, from a central data collection and appraisal office. Among the items reviewed are the person's voluntary records of his outstanding credit transactions, yearly salary to date, taxes, savings, and investments, and amounts of insurance coverage in every line. Additional detailed information on any of the particular items reviewed can be provided by direct connection with any of the financial institutions involved in the case under review.

If the person feels that his situation has changed sufficiently over the past year to cause him to re-evaluate his insurance coverage—or if the computer detects a coverage shortage and indicates to him that there is a deficiency—he can contact an insurance business representative. This representative works for no particular company because the laws forbid use of the central information banks for sales efforts by individual agencies or their salesmen. Instead, the representative works for a central service organization funded as a joint insurance business–government enterprise. The representative calls on the person at an appointed date and time and begins the interview.

On a standard form, the rep enters the coded answers to questions asked of the respondent regarding his income, tax bracket, assets, liabilities, occupation, family situation, property, aspirations, lifestyle, and government-provided coverage. The rep then calls up the central information bank, gets connected with health services, and obtains a full readout of that person's medical history and anticipated health profile.

The rep, using a mini-computer, punches into the terminal all the information gathered in the interview and then calls central insurance. After waiting several minutes for the information to be "processed," the rep receives a print-out with the recommended amounts and types of insurance the individual needs, along with a listing of the companies that sell the coverages recommended, as well as the premium rates for each. Since several types of policies could be recommended, the individual would still contact the company (ies) he finds most satisfactory and arrange to meet with *their* agent(s) in order to make whatever further choices are desired.

Should an individual already be programed with one company (as part of what we now call the life-cycle service), he can use the findings of the business rep to assure himself that his coverage is adequate. Or he can work through his company's agent directly if he has any questions or problems.

•

This work, another product of the Trend Analysis Program, is an instructive one because it takes broader forecasts and imposes them on a single professional area to get a glimpse of what that kind of work could be like in 1990. The same can be done with a little imagination for a host of other professions as well as other elements of our immediate lives. If one takes some of the predicted developments in electronics, energy, and lifestyle and tries to create a typical middle-class household of the future, all sorts of fascinating possibilities can be scripted. For instance, when we have those predicted robots to do cleaning and prepare pre-programed meals, it is easy to write a scenario in which a "human cooked" meal takes on an entirely new significance—perhaps akin to that of the big, once-a-week gourmet meals that some couples dote on today.

3. COMPUTER CONFERENCING SCENARIOS

Although most scenarios are written as a straightforward narrative in which the future is described in the present tense, they take other forms as well. A good case in point is a 1975 study by the Institute for the Future entitled "Group Communications through Computers" in which several variations are used. The gist of the study, conducted for the National Science Foundation, is that computerized conferences—or those held by individuals in different locations through computer networks—are already an important communications medium which will become even more significant in the future. While much of the study involves research and tests of what is now possible, the authors created five scenarios envisioning how the technique will be used five to ten years down the road. Two are common narratives, the other three take the form of an ad in *The New York Times* for August 10, 1983, a letter describing the 1983 "Meeting Without Travel" of the World Future Society and a UPI news story of the same year. The full ad and excerpts from the other two scenarios are quoted to give a feeling for the effectiveness of varying the format and to show the imaginative possibilities of scenario writing.*

Conferencing Unlimited, Inc.

Advertisement   *The New York Times*, August 10, 1983

Conferencing Without Travel

Need to be in touch with people who are far away? Computer conferencing can link you to those people across time and distance barriers. Next time you make a confer-

---

* Notes appended to the ad in the study explain that the company, among other things, had organized the National Basketball Association player draft for 1982, conducted a two-week workshop on "Freedom, Violence and the Law" among the inmates of ten U.S. prisons, and was running the weekly international services for the Psychic Computer Church. As for the company itself, it adds, "Conferencing Unlimited has no central offices; the staff is located in various parts of the world and is interconnected by international computer networks."

ence telephone call or schedule a meeting in a distant place, think about the alternative:

- All arrangements made by our professional staff
- No equipment or technical skills necessary
- Communication through keyboards: you need not be present at the same time as your colleagues, and you'll always have a record of what was said
- Easily accessible anywhere in the United States, Europe, and other areas of the world
- Costs far less than comparable face-to-face meetings

> *"Computer conferencing isn't for everyone, but it might be for you. . . ."*

CALL: CONFERENCE UNLIMITED, INC.
800–987–6543

Letter concerning the "Meeting Without Travel" of the World Future Society of June 3 to July 6, 1983.

Dear Elizabeth:

In the memorandum I sent to your office last week in my capacity as chairman of this year's assembly, I stressed the issues and the substance rather than my experience with the *process* of our meeting. Since that time, however, several people have commented that ours was the first large scientific society to use computer conferencing for a world-wide meeting, and that I would be remiss in my responsibility to our membership if I did not offer an evaluation of this unique experience. Perhaps this letter can be the starting point for such a report if you feel, in your role as president of the society, that my remarks deserve publication.

My first feeling upon emerging from this very intense experience was one of vindication: many of us had complained for years about going to large conferences, about stuffy panels, about lack of participation, and about general frustration. This year's assembly was certainly a far cry from these old hassles.

True, we had our problems, but at least they were *different* problems. The highest percentage of participants were still from the United States, but this time it represented only about 50 percent of the 2,146 registrants. There were more minorities, more women, and more persons from developing countries than at any previous assembly. There was a loud cry that this assembly was more authoritarian than previous meetings; others said it was the most democratic large gathering they had ever attended. Clearly, the meeting was *both* the most authoritarian *and* the most democratic. For electronic gatherings of this sort, the old emphatics seem out of place.

It was authoritarian in those sessions in which leaders exerted a strong control over the proceedings. Some leaders, for instance, limited general input to three lines per message with general participants only allowed a limited number of questions (sometimes they *had* to ask questions, not make comments). These sessions produced orderly transcripts, though in one case, frustrated participants began entering obscene anonymous messages in an attempt to disrupt the meeting. Although this option was rarely used, some participants were forcibly removed from the computer conference. This action by session leaders was, as most of you know by now, highly criticized. (According to assembly rules, no participants could be removed secretly; the whole session was informed when a removal occurred.)

The assembly was more democratic than ever before, in that more complete information was available to more people. Many session leaders allowed full contributions from all attendees (not just from "panelists," who did submit a brief pre-session statement). Content summaries and major conference themes were gathered continuously through computer searches of the text. Where appropriate, samplings of opinion were gathered from all conferees.

Private messages were freely allowed from and to

all participants. Of course, no one was required to answer every private message. However, it does seem that access to well-known persons was higher in this medium and that they could respond easily to a greater number of questions. Synchronous mini-sessions occurred frequently and were often spirited. The apparent impersonality of communicating through computer terminals was balanced by the broad range of interaction which occurred. Casual encounters across continents and between countries took place almost constantly. The global village seemed to come alive, if only for those three weeks.

There is a serious question about whether computer conferences should *replace* more traditional face-to-face assemblies. It is clear that a unique form of communication is possible *without* travel and that this medium should be taken seriously for more regular meetings. The transcripts of sessions were distributed broadly beyond the active participants. (Requests were accepted by mail and were printed on high-speed printers. Whole transcripts could be ordered, as could "keyword" searches, comments by particular persons, or other such selected printings.) A summary of the proceedings was published in paperback form during the week following the conference. Thus, the interaction was high and the circulation broad. We felt as if we were unleashing a monster when the assembly started, and in some sense we were . . .

Wire Service Report on an International Crisis Management Network.

UPI June 2, 1983. The U.S. Senate today voted to officially join the International Crisis Management Network by appointing three U.S. representatives to the network's management board. The act will also provide funding for a staff of U.S. delegates to the network's resource board. The United States has been supporting the ICMN unofficially for the past two years through Department of the Interior funding of its energy-related work. Today's act, when signed by

the President, will transfer the funding responsibility
to the Department of State.

The ICMN is a worldwide network of statespeople
as well as economists, scientists, military strategists,
psychologists and other resource persons who are connected to a twenty-four-hour-a-day computer conferencing service. The ICMN was established two years
ago when three major international planning networks
merged. These earlier networks had been designed to
promote international cooperation in energy distribution, food distribution, and trade, respectively. But
while even these networks were well attended by representatives of most Western nations, the Soviet Union,
Japan, and Australia, the ICMN has not until recently
been officially recognized by any state, and its decisions and recommendations have thus not been bind-
ing.

Nevertheless, the ICMN has been uniquely successful in dealing with a number of worldwide crises.
Typically, crisis negotiations involve intensive, synchronous network sessions. During these sessions, the
members of the management board are almost continuously at their computer terminals. The negotiations
have often been characterized as tidal waves of information: negotiators depend heavily on extensive information exchange with their own resource people
as well as with those of other nations. Some researchers
estimate that computer conferencing allows the exchange of this information about five times faster than
face-to-face meetings in highly structured environments such as the United Nations—a point demonstrated by its swift handling of the "portable H-bomb"
international scare of last year . . .

4. UNPREDICTABLE TURNING POINTS IN WORLD HISTORY: 1975–1995 (A FEW EXAMPLES)

These scenarios, of which there are many more, were
delivered for the use of the Panel on Science, Environment
and Technology of the Senate Public Works Committee by

William H. Overholt of the Hudson Institute in 1976, slightly updating an earlier collection done in 1972. The purpose of the exercise is to envision a series of surprises possible in the years ahead paralleling such past surprises as Pearl Harbor, the Nixon visit to China, and the Arab oil boycott. Their intended worth is in keeping people alert to the possibility of low-probability events.

The importance of this kind of scenario writing was underscored in the introductory note to the 1976 version of the paper in which it was acknowledged by the author that a number of "unlikely but important" events had come true since 1972 when the original paper was written including the explosion of an Indian A-bomb, the rise of Italian communism, the sudden unification of Vietnam, growing crises in South Africa and Rhodesia, and threats to the cohesion of NATO.

TURNING POINT 8: Ascension to power of a fanatical regime in the USSR or China.

SCENARIO A: [Written before Mao's death] China has undergone several major leftist upheavals including the Great Leap Forward and the Cultural Revolution. It is currently undergoing an anti-Confucian campaign, which is probably an attack by the fanatical left on some of the senior figures in the Chinese regime. Given the ideological character of the anti-Confucianist movement, it may even be an attack on Chairman Mao from the left. One may at least reasonably hypothesize the possibility that, following the death of Chairman Mao, an extreme leftist group of this kind might rise to power for a shorter or longer period in Peking and attack first Quemoy and Matsu and then Taiwan and later involve itself militarily in Laos or elsewhere. Conceivably such a regime could frighten Vietnam into an extreme pro-Soviet stance, and such a stance in turn could provoke Chinese intervention in North Vietnam.

SCENARIO B: Sino-Soviet war, and particularly a prolonged Sino-Soviet war, could put great strain on the Soviet Union and on its eastern European bloc. Revolts in various parts of the Soviet Union and perhaps also in eastern European countries like Poland and Czechoslovakia could conceivably bring to power a fanatical regime in the Kremlin which would exploit all available weaponry and undertake any politcal/military strategy which seemed to offer some chance for survival of the Soviet regime—even at the cost of risking World War III or devastation of much of the world or both.

TURNING POINT 25: Catastrophic nuclear accident.

SCENARIO: The energy crisis intensifies and becomes extremely severe. As a result, several nations rush headlong into construction of breeder reactors and modify some of what come to seem like excessively severe constraints on reactor construction. After one New York reactor is installed, but before construction of the entire plant is completed, a fire breaks out and a small explosion occurs. Small amounts of plutonium blow over nearby New York City, inducing long-term crippling or fatal diseases in thousands of people. The reactor [then] explodes, killing a million people and spreading damage over a large area.

TURNING POINT 26: Successful resolution of the Arab-Israeli conflict.

SCENARIO: Following a war so damaging and unsatisfactory in outcome to both sides that motivations for long-term settlement become very strong, the Israelis and the Arabs negotiate a gradual series of compromises in which Israel gives back much of the Arab territory conquered in 1967 in return for which the Arabs agree to withdraw their armed forces from any area near Israel. Both sides agree to at very substantial disarmament program, and the great powers facilitate success of this part of the agreement by providing military guarantees in the area and by refusing to sell more than small volumes of arms to countries in the region.

4

THE WORST PREDICTIONS

Or, Why to Beware the Bathtub

In the fall of 1976 I saw a press release from the U.S. Department of the Interior which said that scientific evidence collected by that agency indicated that winters were not getting colder as others had claimed. Within a few months we were in the grip of the bone-chilling winter of 1977, and as I was strolling across the frozen Potomac from Maryland to Virginia (an opportunity last afforded to pedestrians in button shoes) the point hit home that people are forever recalling how so-and-so predicted this or that with uncanny accuracy, but that bad predictions tend to get forgotten. For example, there are few people who have not heard President Eisenhower's famous prediction/ warning about the growing power of the "military-industrial complex," but how many recall a speech he made at West Point in 1967 in which he proclaimed, "Whatever happens in Vietnam, I can conceive of nothing except military victory"? Many have written about the prescience of Jules Verne and H. G. Wells, but how seldom are their errors recalled? Most schoolchildren are aware of Verne's vision of the submarine, but how often do we hear Wells's later prediction from his book *Anticipations?* He wrote, "I must confess that my imagination, in spite even of spurring, refuses to see any sort of submarine doing anything but suffocating its crew and floundering at sea."

Often the totally wrong predictions are more fascinating

than those which are right on target for the simple reason that they show how wrong the experts can be.

The sheer volume of bad predictions is such that one is hard-pressed to know where to begin. Without much effort, for example, one could compile a collection of bad predictions by noted Americans on the outcome of the war in Vietnam large enough to fill a fair-sized book. Come to think of it, one could probably put a companion volume together on the earlier predictions by French leaders on their coming victory in Indo-China. There have been so many lousy predictions in the field of medicine that a multivolume collection would be no problem, and the resulting work would be liberally sprinkled with hilarious examples such as quotes from those who argued that the smallpox vaccination would create a race of humans with hairy, cowlike faces (after all, the word vaccinate *does* come from the Latin word for cow, *vacca*).

Even an innovation as simple as the bathtub had its own set of absurd forecasts. A few years ago a researcher at the Library of Congress was collecting bad predictions of all kinds and found this quotation in a 1926 *New York Times* feature: "In the 1840s the bathtub was denounced in the United States as an epicurian innovation from England designed to corrupt the democratic simplicity of the Republic. The medical profession warned against it as a producer of rheumatic fevers, inflammatory lungs and all zymotic diseases." *The Times* could hardly be too smug about the bathtub forecasts because it had published its own share of bad predictions including editorials proclaiming attempts to fly a waste of time and money (this is 1903, just before the Wright Brothers flight) and another telling rocket pioneer Robert Goddard that even a high school student had enough knowledge to know that a rocket could not fly in space. In July, 1969, as Apollo 11 was about to make its lunar landing, *The Times* ran a correction noting. "It is now definitely established that a rocket can function in a vacuum. *The Times* regrets the error."

In retrospect, the funniest bad predictions are the hysterical kind like those which attached themselves to the bathtub, but conservative forecasts often carry greater irony. Back in the early 1950s, when the first pioneering Univac 1 computer was delivered to the U.S. Bureau of the Census, the experts in the new field of computing machines sat down and predicted a market for computers of all types soon reaching several dozen. They added that by 1970 there would be no less than 100 computers in the United States. In 1970 the American computer population fell just short of 200,000 units. Another good example of this type was that of the management consulting firm which told General Motors just after World War I that it should dump its Chevrolet division because the company could not hope to make a success out of this car. Similarly, a Midwest utility offered Henry Ford a good job if he would stop working with his gasoline engine and devote himself to something useful. The list goes on: aviation pioneer Octave Chanute predicted that the only important use that lay ahead for the airplane was for sport; Winston Churchill was told by Lord Cherwell that the Nazis' threat to unleash V-2 bombs on London was just a meaningless publicity stunt; Lord Rutherford, who was once the world's leading expert on nuclear physics, maintained until his death in 1937 that the concept of releasing atomic energy was "pure moonshine." Arthur C. Clarke has encountered so many of these conservative predictions over the years that he came up with an observation on the phenomenon which has come to be known as "Clarke's Law." It states, "When a distinguished but elderly scientist states something is possible, he is almost certainly right. When he states that something is impossible, he is very probably wrong."

Because of the abundance of bad predictions, it is not hard to come up with a collection of stunning ones. Here are some of the author's favorites collected from a number of sources.*

* The best and most extensive collection I have seen is contained in a 1969 report by Nancy Gamarra of the Library of Congress entitled "Erroneous Predictions and Negative Comments Concerning Exploration, Territorial Expansion, Scientific and Technological Development; Selected Statements." It was published by the Library's Legislative Reference Service.

The A-Bomb

"That is the biggest fool thing we have ever done . . . The bomb will never go off, and I speak as an expert in explosives."

—Admiral William Leahy's comments to President Harry Truman

The Airplane

"The example of the bird does not prove that man can fly . . . There are many problems which have fascinated mankind since civilization began, which we have made little or no advance in solving . . . May not our mechanisms . . . be ultimately forced to admit that aerial flight is one of that great class of problems with which man can never cope, and give up all attempts to grapple with it? . . . Imagine the proud possessor of the aeroplane darting through the air at a speed of several hundred feet per second! Is it the speed alone that sustains him? How is he ever going to stop? . . . The construction of an aerial vehicle which could carry even a single man from place to place at pleasure requires the discovery of some new metal or some new force. Even with such a discovery we could not expect one to do more than carry its owner."

—Simon Newcomb, the astronomer, published in October, 1903, just two months prior to the Wright Brothers' initial flight

Alaska

"In support of the proposition of the utter worthlessness of this territory there are several general tests of a most important and convincing character. Conclusive proof of it is that Russia would sell her territory . . . if it was not valuable to her, it will never prove any value to us. Russia is not a power to surrender a foothold upon earth unless it should be an actual and annoying burden to her."

—Representative John A. Peters, 1868; one of a number of dire predictions regarding the purchase of Alaska

American Society

"I thank God there are no free schools, nor printing, and I hope we shall not have them these hundred years; for learning has brought disobedience and heresy and sects into the world, and printing has divulged them and libels against the best government."

—*Governor William Berkeley,*
Virginia, 1670

American Youth

"We are gradually approaching, with the decadence of youth, a near proximity to a nation of madmen. By comparing the lunacy statistics of 1809 with those of 1909 . . . an insane world is looked forward to by me with a certainty in the not far distant future."

—*Winslow Forbes, M.D., 1910*

Artificial Life

"[One hundred years hence] . . . man will be so completely the master of organic law that he would create life in competition with God."

—*Claude Bernard, 1869*

The Automobile

"The ordinary 'horsless carriage' is at present a luxury for the wealthy; and although its price will probably fall in the future, it will never, of course, come into as common use as the bicycle."

—THE LITERARY DIGEST,
October 14, 1899

"[After motor cars come into common use] we shall probably find public taste changing so that many people will prefer to travel from place to place more slowly than at present."

—*from the article "Automobiles*
for the Average Man" by Cleveland
Moffett from REVIEW OF REVIEWS,
June, 1900.

Bolshevism

"What are the Bolsheviki? They are representatives of the most democratic government in Europe . . . Let us recognize the truest democracy in Europe, the truest democracy in the world today."

—*William Randolph Hearst,*
1918

Capitalism

"Capitalism is dying, and its extremities are already decomposing. The blotches upon the surface show that the blood no longer circulates. The time is near when the cadaver will have to be removed and the atmosphere purified."

—*Eugene V. Debs, 1904*

Commercial Television

"While theoretically and technically television may be feasible, commercially and financially I consider it an impossibility, a development of which we need waste little time dreaming."

—*Lee DeForest, 1926*

Communications

"Within the memory of this generation, the earth has been girdled with iron and steel, and the electric telegraph and the cable have practically annihilated terrestrial space; these modes of communication have come to stay, and they are ultimate."

—THE ATLANTIC MONTHLY, *1902*

Electricity in the Home

"Just as certain as death, [George] Westinghouse will kill a customer within six months after he puts in a system of any size."

—*Thomas Edison, quoted in*
MEN OF SCIENCES AND INVENTIONS

The Grand Canyon

"[It] . . . is, of course, altogether valueless . . . Ours has been the first, and will doubtless be the last, party of whites to visit this profitless locality. It seems intended by nature that the Colorado River . . . shall be forever unvisited and undisturbed."

—Lieutenant Joseph C. Ives, Corps of Topographical Engineers, 1861

Highways

"The actual building of roads devoted to motor cars is not for the near future, in spite of many rumors to that effect."

—HARPERS WEEKLY, *August 2, 1902*

Inventions

"The advancement of the arts from year to year taxes our credulity and seems to presage the arrival of that period when further improvement must end."

—Henry L. Ellsworth, U.S. Commissioner of Patents, 1844

Jet Propulsion

"The proposals as outlined in your letter . . . have been carefully reviewed . . . While the Air Corps is deeply interested in the research work being carried out by your organization . . . it does not, at this time, feel justified in obligating further funds for basic jet propulsion research and experimentation . . ."

—Letter from the Army to Robert Goddard, the father of American rocketry

Moon Landing

"Landing and moving around the moon offers so many serious problems for human beings that it may take science another 200 years to lick them."

SCIENCE DIGEST, *August, 1948*

Rock 'n' Roll Music

"If we cannot stem the tide of rock 'n' roll with its waves of rhythmic narcosis and of future waves of vicarious craze, we are preparing our own downfall in the midst of pandemonic funeral dances."

> —Dr. A. M. Meerio, Associate
> Professor of Psychiatry at
> Columbia University (quoted
> in THE NEW YORK TIMES,
> February 23, 1957)

Rocketry

"That Professor Goddard with his 'chair' in Clark College and the countenancing of the Smithsonian does not know the relation of action to reaction, and of the need to have something better than a vacuum against which to react—to say that would be absurd. Of course he only seems to lack the knowledge ladled out daily in high schools . . ."

> —NEW YORK TIMES editorial
> of January 13, 1920

The Screw Propeller

". . . even if the propeller had the power of propelling a vessel, it would be found altogether useless in practice, *because* the power being applied in the *stern* it would be *absolutely impossible* to make the vessel steer."

> —Sir William Symonds,
> Surveyor of the British Navy,
> 1837

Social Impact of Air Travel

"There is one more progress to be realized . . . to find the means of guiding in a mass of air a lighter bubble than air . . . That very instant frontiers vanish, barriers are effaced; the entire Chinese Wall around thought, around commerce, around industry, around nationalities, around progress falls down . . . No more hatreds, no more self-interests devouring one another, no more wars; a new life made up of harmony and light prevails."

> —Victor Hugo, 1842

Social Impact of Air Travel (Part II)

"[The development of the flying machine] will be a happy dawn for earth-dwellers, for war will become so destructive that it will probably bring its own end; and the human caterpillar, already mechanically converted into the grasshopper, will become a fairly beautiful butterfly."

—John Jacob Astor, 1903

Surgery

"The abdomen, the chest, and the brain will be forever shut from the intrusion of the wise and humane surgeon."

—Sir John Erichsen, 1873

On the Telegraph and Samuel F. B. Morse

"I watched his countenance closely, to see if he was not deranged . . . and I was assured by other Senators after we left the room that they had no confidence in it."

—Senator Smith of Indiana on Morse's display of the telegraph before Congress, 1842

Urban Sprawl

"Philadelphia will be a suburb of New York in twenty years."

—William Baldwin, President of the Long Island Railraod, 1903

Urban Transportation

". . . surface travel will be an oddity [in New York] in twenty years."

—John B. McDonald, the builder of New York's first subway, 1903

Venus

"I can tell from here . . . what the inhabitants of Venus are like; they resemble the Moors of Granada: a small, black people, burned by the sun, full of wit and fire, always in love, writing verse, fond of music, arranging festivals, dances and tournaments every day."

—*Bernard de Fontenelle, 1686*

Wireless Communications

"You could put in this room . . . all the radio-telephone apparatus that the country will ever need."

—*W. W. Dean, president of
the Dean Telephone Co., 1907*

War

"[Before] the 20th century closes, the earth will be purged of its foulest shame, the killing of men in battle under the name of war."

—*Andrew Carnegie, 1901*

Warships

"As far as sinking a ship with a bomb is concerned, you just can't do it."

—*Rear Admiral Clark Woodward,
USN, 1939*

World Collapse

"My figures coincide in fixing 1950 as the year when the world must go smash."

—*Henry Adams, 1903*

5

BRAVE
NEW WORDS
It's One Thing to Think Like a Futurist,
Another to Sound Like One

Anyone who has ever attended a futures conference at
which leading practitioners of the art hold forth—or read
some of their books—is aware of the fact that futurism
has its own vocabulary. Excluding some of those like
Delphi and *surprise-free scenario*, which have already
been discussed in some detail, here is an alphabetized collection of other terms in vogue in futures circles. It is not
meant to be a comprehensive listing but rather a healthy
sampling.

Ad-hocracy—A term created by Alvin Toffler in *Future Shock* to describe teams accomplishing work on an
ad hoc basis. Toffler believes the ad-hocracy is the organization of the future which will ultimately supplement
the bureaucracy.

Appropriate Technology—That which fits the existing
needs of a local population rather than "state of the art"
technology which attempts to reshape those needs. Appropriate technologies are typically those which conserve
energy and resources, are inexpensive and easily maintained. Also referred to as intermediate, soft, and alternative technology.

Artificial Intelligence—A machine capable of learning
and reasoning.

Boswash—Term for the growing Super-city between
Boston and Washington. Has also been called Bosnywash,

Atlantic Strip City, and Northeast Corridor. Herman Kahn, who coined the term "Boswash," has since suggested that Portport might be a better name as Boswash may eventually extend from Portsmouth, Virginia, to Portland, Maine.

Chipitts—Name being used to describe the Super-city developing along the strip between Chicago and Pittsburgh. Also called GLM for Great Lakes Megalopolis.

Cyberneticians—A coming human elite that will have rapport with advanced computers. Donald Michael, the man who coined the term, says, "These cyberneticians will have established a relationship with their machines that cannot be shared with the average man, any more than the average man today can understand the problems of molecular biology, nuclear physics, or neuropsychiatry."

Cyborgs—Humans fitted with a large number of mechanical or electronic replacement parts à la the Bionic Woman.

Discontinuity—A radical shift in direction or trend such as when we we are told that rural America is declining in population and we pick up *The New York Times* one day and read that all the experts were stunned to learn that the rural population has expanded by a cool million in recent years (a real discontinuity reported in *The Times*, February 27, 1977).

The Doomsday Syndrome—Term coined by British science editor John Maddox in a book of the same name. It refers to the trend in which a condition or problem (pollution, population, food, energy, etc.) is extrapolated into a forecast of catastrophe. It has also been called the "doom boom."

Dystopia—A negative future, the opposite of utopia, such as *1984* or *Rollerball*. "Anti-utopia" is another term used to describe this state.

Econometrics—Equations or models which describe the working of an economy.

Electronic Funds Transfer (EFT)—The current term for automated financial transactions of which today's robot bank tellers are just the beginning. Its ultimate extension is the "cashless, checkless society," in which credit, payments, interest, savings, purchases, and salaries are all matters of electronics.

Fixed Pie—The view of the world which says we know the earth's limits for production and resources. The contrasting view is that of the "growing pie," which says that with the help of technology the earth is capable of producing much more.

Futuristics—The preferred term for the study of the future used by those who object to the term "futurology" because the suffix "-ology" implies the study of something which already exists.

Futurizing—The process by which an outlook or institution is reoriented toward the future. A World Future Society document explains it by applying it to education. "Futurizing a curriculum . . . is different from merely updating it. It signifies a general commitment to make education relevant to the student's future."

Genius Forecasting—Misnomer since it refers to the intuitive forecast of any expert or "inspired" individual. H. G. Wells fits the category, but so does Henry Ford, who made a lot of forecasts that never came true.

Gulf City—Name in use for the Super-city that will extend from Miami to Houston. Also called the Coastal Crescent.

Heuristic—Describes a device created to stimulate further thought. A scenario depicting the collapse of the U.S. government can be used heuristically to get people to think more about the strengths and weaknesses of the government.

Holistic—A very popular term for describing the wholeness of something—as in "a holistic view of the future"—from the Greek *holos*, for "complete." Futurists never spell it wholistic and look down their noses at those who do.

Interactive Video—TV systems in which the viewer can talk back, such as situations in which we will be able to react to a policy matter by signaling a "yea" or "nay" from our living rooms.

Lifeboat Ethic—The moral code based on the belief that an individual or nation can justify not aiding less fortunate individuals or nations.

Long-Term Multifold Trend—The collective list of individual trends which describe the direction of Western civilization. In the book *Things to Come,* co-authors Herman Kahn and Barry Bruce-Briggs list fifteen key elements of the larger trend ranging from "Centralization and concentration of economic and political power" to "Population growth." Perhaps the most important question now being discussed by those looking at the future of values is whether or not the LTMT is going to stay on track or go through a transformation.

The Mature Society—Dennis Gabor's term for a society that bases its choices on rational, scientific wisdom rather than prejudice and emotion. In Gabor's view such a society will be able to provide a moderate level of affluence within the framework of a low-growth economy.

Neo-Malthusian—Modern thinker who sees population growing faster than the availability of resources to support them.

Nuclear Dyad—Spiffy futuristic term for the childless husband and wife, as opposed to the nuclear family which has offspring.

Paradigm—An old word for pattern or model which has been rescued from obscurity by futures researchers who use it commonly to describe a set of values and behavior patterns (e.g., the industrial paradigm vs. the post-industrial paradigm).

Pluralistic Society—One in which a various number of groups (racial, economic, social, religious, etc.) are able to maintain both identity and some degree of autonomy, as opposed to a homogeneous society. A number of futures researchers believe that America is becoming increasingly pluralistic.

Population Bulge—A sophisticated term for the "baby boom" which came after World War II.

Post-Affluence—The period of lowered living standards which many believe is now at hand. The period will be typified by new scarcities and the need to learn thrifty habits. It contrasts to the period of affluence which ran from 1945 through 1970.

Post-Attack Economy—A fancy term for the America

that will exist after a nuclear interchange (if there are enough people left to maintain an economy).

Pro-Act—To respond in advance, the opposite of react.

Psychology of Entitlement—The process by which one's wants are turned into perceived social rights—for instance, the desire to be well housed becoming the right to good housing. The term was coined by Daniel Yankelovich.

Railway Thinking—That way of thinking about the future in which history is seen as something which repeats itself. It is often applied to nations by those who assume that the stages an advanced nation goes through will be repeated, eventually, by lesser-developed ones.

Sansan—One name for the Super-city being created as everything from San Francisco to San Diego sprawls and merges. Other names: the California Strip, Pacific City, and California Megalopolis.

Self-Fulfilling Prophecy—A statement that tends to make itself come true because it has been uttered. E.g., if it is said that Tampa is the fastest-growing city in the country and that encourages a lot of companies to relocate there, the prophecy is then realized.

Social Indicator—A statistic or set of statistics which serves as a barometer for the state of society. For example, analysts working for the city of New York have used the number of false alarms set off within an area to indicate the level of dissatisfaction and alienation within that section of the city.

Spaceship Ethic—Moral code based on the concept of the earth as a large spaceship on which survival depends on the cooperation and coordination of all the passengers.

Suitcase War—That state (which many say we are fast approaching) in which devastating nuclear, biological, chemical, or other forms of weapon can be carried to a city or military center by a single person and unleashed.

SYNCON—or SYNergistic CONvergence. A process developed by the Committee for the Future in which experts and a cross-section of local residents are brought together to solve problems and plan for the future. It stresses resolving conflicts without developing adversary relationships.

Technetronic Society—Zbigniew Brzezinski's term for a future state in which a technocratic elite works full-time to run the system while the mass population is freed from labor by technology for leisured pursuits.

Time Horizon—The furthest into the future that one plans for and considers. IBM certainly has a greater time horizon than a marginally profitable maker of curtains.

The Titanic Analogy—The comparison of the present world situation to that of the "unsinkable" *Titanic*. The term is used by those who feel that we are unable to prevent catastrophe because of the prevailing thought which says we are unsinkable.

Transadulthood—A name for a new stage in the life cycle: the period which extends from the end of adolescence into the late twenties or early thirties, when one experiments with lifestyles. Adulthood follows.

Transnational—Corporations that transcend the ties of a home country and become sovereign states unto themselves. They will be unlike the old-fashioned multinationals which are linked to a mother country.

Up-Wingers—F. M. Esfandiary's term from a book of the same title which refers to people who are neither left- nor right-wing, but apolitically futurized.

Wargasm—The condition which occurs when all nuclear and thermonuclear buttons get pushed. Another term attributed to the fertile mind of Herman Kahn.

Wild Card—The term used to describe a major, unforeseen development that could wipe out less dramatic scenarios and projections. A nuclear holocaust, the total downfall of civilization in its present form, a worldwide totalitarian state, and extraterrestrial invasion are all wild cards. Corporate and government planners usually shy away from wild cards simply because they usually spell the end of corporations and governments.

INDEX

AVON   THE BEST IN
BESTSELLING ENTERTAINMENT